W9-DCJ-779

UBU REPERTORY THEATER PUBLICATIONS

Individual plays

* *Swimming Pools at War* by Yves Navarre, 1982.
* *Night Just Before the Forest* and *Struggle of the Dogs and the Black,* by Bernard-Marie Koltès, 1982.
* *The Fetishist* by Michel Tournier, 1983.
* *The Office* by Jean-Paul Aron, 1983.
* *Far From Hagondange* and *Vater Land, the Country of our Fathers* by Jean-Paul Wenzel, 1984.
* *Deck Chairs* by Madeleine Laïk, 1984.
* *The Passport* and *The Door* by Pierre Bourgeade, 1984.
* *The Showman* by Andrée Chedid, 1984.
* *Madame Knipper's Journey to Eastern Prussia* by Jean-Luc Lagarce, 1984.
  Family Portrait by Denise Bonal, 1985; new edition, 1992.
* *Passengers* by Daniel Besnehard, 1985.
* *Cabale* by Enzo Cormann, 1985.
  Enough is Enough by Protais Asseng, 1986.
  Monsieur Thôgô-gnigni by Bernard Dadié, 1985.
  The Glorious Destiny of Marshal Nnikon Nniku by Tchicaya U Tam'si, 1986.
  Parentheses of Blood by Sony Labou Tansi, 1986.
  Intelligence Powder by Kateb Yacine, 1986.
  The Sea Between Us by Denise Chalem, 1986.
  Country Landscapes by Jacques-Pierre Amette, 1986.
  Nowhere and *A Man with Women* by Reine Bartève, 1987.
  The White Bear by Daniel Besnehard, 1992.
  The Best of Schools by Jean-Marie Besset, 1992.
  Jock by Jean-Louis Bourdon, 1992.
  A Tempest by Aimé Césaire, 1993 (new edition).
  The Free Zone and *The Workroom* by Jean-Claude Grumberg, preface by Michael R. Marrus, 1993.

Ubu Repertory Theater:1982-1992, A bilingual illustrated history with personal statements by various playwrights and theater personalities, 1992.

* *Distributed by Ubu Repertory Theater, 15 West 28th Street, New York, NY 10001. All other titles distributed by Theatre Communications Group, 355 Lexington Avenue, New York, NY 10017.*

Anthologies

Afrique I: New plays from the Congo, Ivory Coast, Senegal and Zaire, including *The Daughter of the Gods* by Abdou Anta Kâ, *Equatorium* by Maxime N'Debeka, *Lost Voices* by Diur N'Tumb, *The Second Ark* by Sony Labou Tansi, and *The Eye* by Bernard Zadi Zaourou. Preface by George C. Wolfe. 1987. (Out of print).

The Paris Stage: Recent Plays: *A Birthday Present for Stalin* by Jean Bouchaud, *The Rest Have Got It Wrong* by Jean-Michel Ribes, *The Sleepless City* by Jean Tardieu, *Trumpets of Death* by Tilly, and *The Neighbors* by Michel Vinaver. Preface by Catherine Temerson and Françoise Kourilsky. 1988.

Plays by Women: An International Anthology: *A Picture Perfect Sky* by Denise Bonal, *Jocasta* by Michèle Fabien, *The Girls from the Five and Ten* by Abla Farhoud, *You Have Come Back* by Fatima Gallaire-Bourega, and *Your Handsome Captain* by Simone Schwarz-Bart. Preface by Catherine Temerson and Françoise Kourilsky. 1988, 1991. (Out of print).

Gay Plays: An International Anthology: *The Function* by Jean-Marie Besset, *A Tower Near Paris* and *Grand Finale* by Copi, *Return of the Young Hippolytus* by Hervé Dupuis, *Ancient Boys* by Jean-Claude van Itallie, and *The Lives and Deaths of Miss Shakespeare* by Liliane Wouters. Preface by Catherine Temerson and Françoise Kourilsky. 1989, 1991.

Theater and Politics: An International Anthology: *Black Wedding Candles for Blessed Antigone* by Sylvain Bemba, *A Season in the Congo* by Aimé Césaire, *Burn River Burn* by Jean-Pol Fargeau, *Olympe and the Executioner* by Wendy Kesselman and *Mephisto*, adapted from Klaus Mann by Ariane Mnouchkine. Preface by Erika Munk. 1990.

Afrique II: New Plays from Madagascar, Mauritania and Togo including *The Legend of Wagadu as Seen by Sia Yatabere* by Moussa Diagana, *The Crossroads* by Josué Kossi Efoui, *The Herd* by Charlotte-Arrisoa Rafenomanjato, *The Prophet and the President* by Jean-Luc Raharimanana and *The Singing Tortoise* and *Yevi's Adventures in Monsterland* by Sénouvo Agbota Zinsou. Preface by Henry Louis Gates, Jr. 1991.

New French Language Plays: *The Orphan Muses* by Michel Marc Bouchard (Quebec), *Fire's Daughters* by Ina Césaire (Martinique), *The Ship* by Michèle Césaire (Martinique), *Talk About Love!* by Paul Emond (Belgium), *That Old Black Magic* by Koffi Kwahulé (Ivory Coast). Preface by Rosette C. Lamont. 1993.

Plays by Women: An International Anthology, Book 2: *The Orphanage* by Reine Bartève (France), *Game of Patience* by Abla Farhoud (Quebec), *The Widow Dylemma* by Werewere Liking (Cameroon), *The Tropical Breeze Hotel* by Maryse Condé (Guadeloupe), *Beware the Heart* by Denise Bonal (France). Preface by Ntozake Shange. 1994.

AN INTERNATIONAL ANTHOLOGY

plays by

WOMEN

BOOK TWO

Preface by

NTOZAKE SHANGE

UBU REPERTORY THEATER PUBLICATIONS
NEW YORK

CAUTION

These plays are fully protected by copyright. All rights are reserved. All inquiries concerning the rights for professional or amateur stage productions should be made as follows:

For *The Orphanage:* Société des Auteurs et Compositeurs Dramatiques (SACD), Promotion des Répertoires et de l'Action Culturelle, 11 bis rue Ballu, 75009 Paris, France. Tel.: (1) 40.23.44.44.

For *Game of Patience:* Marie-Francine Des Landes, Des Landes, Dickinson et associés, 4171 avenue Hampton, Montréal, Quebec, Canada H4A 2L1.

For *The Widow Dylemma:* Claire Laroche de Féline, 5 Boulevard d'Indochine, 75019 Paris, France. Tel.: (1) 42.41.84.64.

For *The Tropical Breeze Hotel:* Société des Auteurs et Compositeurs Dramatiques (SACD), Promotion des Répertoires et de l'Action Culturelle, 11 bis rue Ballu, 75009 Paris, France. Tel.: (1) 40.23.44.44.

For *Beware the Heart:* Société des Auteurs et Compositeurs Dramatiques (SACD), Promotion des Répertoires et de l'Action Culturelle, 11 bis rue Ballu, 75009 Paris, France. Tel.: (1) 40.23.44.44.

Ubu Repertory Theater Publications
General Editors: Françoise Kourilsky, Catherine Temerson
Assistant Editor: Cristina Strempel

Distributed by Theatre Communications Group, 355 Lexington Avenue, New York, NY 10017

Price: $ 15.95
Printed in the United States of America 1994
Library of Congress Catalog Card Number: 89-142722
ISBN 0-913745-42-1

CONTENTS

PREFACE

From de Staël to de Beauvoir, Sand to Colette, the woman's voice in French literature is invariably pearl smooth, white and sophisticated. The worldliness afforded Francophone women by the sheer vastness of the territories eludes the woman of color who could not go abroad to see herself; could not find the exotic in what for her was commonplace. Her voice from Guadeloupe to Algiers, Saigon and Dakar is undeciphered, cloaked in sugar cane and sexuality: Josephine Baker wore bananas in the dead of winter. Our instincts are inappropriate in metro Paris. Who would know what we are trying to say. The woman of color slipping her tongue around the sounds that enforced our bondage, insured our abandonment in the hinterlands of racism, is now assembled in this anthology from Ubu Repertory Theater in all her glory and ferocity.

Because so little is known of our desires and dreams, these plays are marvelously idiosyncratic, eccentric, and brimming over with passion, humor, and the odyssey caused by the kneading of language, the melding of Arabic and Creole through the history that is French, forever confounding, and dazzling. As Abla Farhoud writes in *Game of Patience:*

> "Go on with your solitaire if you like, but don't interrupt me. In a country with no name and no borders, a little girl was born."

That little girl is any one of us determined to find the words that reflect the world, our worlds, as we experience ourselves. This collection brings us into lives vehemently lived and warmly remembered.

NTOZAKE SHANGE

REINE BARTEVE

THE ORPHANAGE

Translated from the French by

JILL MAC DOUGALL

UBU REPERTORY THEATER PUBLICATIONS
NEW YORK

Reine Bartève enjoys a wide–ranging career in the theater both as an actress and a playwright. She has appeared in classical roles as well as in productions of Anouilh, Ionesco, and Tennessee Williams. She wrote her first play, *L'Arménoche (Nowhere)* in 1975. It was produced in Paris in 1976, and has since enjoyed many revivals. In 1985 Françoise Kourilsky directed its American premiere, entitled *Nowhere,* at La Mama. The play was given a new production at Ubu Rep in 1992, also directed by Françoise Kourilsky. Bartève has written more than twelve new plays since *L'Arménoche,* including *Le Pavillon Balthazar, Ouverture sur mer* and, in 1984, *L'Orphelinat (The Orphanage),* all of which have been produced in Paris. Her adaptation of Balzac's *Le Père Goriot* aired on French radio in 1990. *Vivre la nuit (Alive by Night),* commissioned by the French government for the Bicentennial of the French Revolution, was produced in English in 1989 by Ubu Rep and staged in French in Verdun the same year. Bartève was awarded a grant from the Beaumarchais Foundation for her most recent play, *Le Désir du figuier.* She has also received grants from the French Ministry of Culture and the Centre National des Lettres.

Jill Mac Dougall has been active in directing productions and conducting workshops, in translating plays, and in performance research in Europe, Africa and North America for over twenty years. Her translations for Ubu include *The Eye* (Bernard Zadi Zaourou), *The Girls from the 5 and 10* (Abla Farhoud), *Lost Voices* (Diur N'Tumb), *You Have Come Back* (Fatima Gallaire-Bourega), *Burn River Burn* (Jean–Pol Fargeau), *The Crossroads* (Josué Kossi Efoui) and *That Old Black Magic* (Koffi Kwahulé) all published in the series Ubu Repertory Theater Publications. She holds a Ph.D. in Performance Studies (NYU) and is presently teaching acting and theatre history with Pennsylvania State University.
The translation of *The Orphanage* was made possible by a grant from the National Theater Translation Fund.

The Orphanage, in Jill Mac Dougall's translation, had its American premiere at Ubu Repertory Theater, 15 West 28th Street, New York, NY 10001, on April 5th, 1994.

Director: ....**Françoise Kourilsky**
Set Designer: ....**Watoku Ueno**
Lighting Designer: ....**Greg MacPherson**
Costume Designer: ....**Carol Ann Pelletier**
Music composed and performed by: ....**Mauro Refosco**

CAST, IN ORDER OF APPEARANCE

Mado. ....**Tanya Lopert**
Azaf ....**Chad L. Coleman**
Gwen ....**Julie Boyd**
Makuma ....**La Tonya Borsay**
Nesilili ....**Markita Prescott**
Zugrako ....**Eric Coleman**

Produced by **Ubu Repertory Theater**
Françoise Kourilsky, *Artistic Director.*

AUTHOR'S NOTE

What memories are buried in my mind, of stifled cries, hidden tears, and hushed words grownups utter while bent over some photographs. In trembling voices they tell the dreadful story of orphans: lost, found, disappeared children. What images of my past as an Armenian child burst forth during a long African tour of *Antigone*... The rebellious cries of Antigone—the orphan and outlaw I incarnated every evening on the stage in African cities and villages—fused with my memory and what I was witnessing. Then, one morning in March, I and some of my fellow actors visited an orphanage...

The courtyard. Small children sitting in a circle or lying on the ground. Some standing against the great wall of the orphanage. Silent. Motionless. The fierce gaze of prisoners, dark with suffering.

When I got back to France, still under the shock of that immediate reality and the past it had brought to life in me, I wrote *The Orphanage*. The characters which emerged are gripped by the cruel passions and extravagant dreams of lost souls, abandoned and humiliated. Some are possessed by their ideals of justice; others by their love of money. Prisoners of their contradictions, they clash head on in one intense moment which becomes a life or death struggle.

REINE BARTEVE

CHARACTERS

MADO FORGUS, *European owner of the Artistic Hotel, in her early fifties.*

GWEN, *European visitor at the hotel, in her early thirties.*

AZAF, *Mado's employee, handsome African in his late twenties.*

ZUGRAKO, *The African chief of police, Mado's lover, in his forties or fifties.*

MAKUMA, *A young African woman working for Mado.*

NESILILI, *A frail African girl of around five.*

SCENE 1

Late afternoon.
At the Artistic Hotel, somewhere in Africa.

Mado is seated at a table, shifting through papers. She is smoking as she goes through the bills. Azaf stands next to her. He is wiping wine glasses.

MADO: She hasn't gone out?

AZAF: No, she's in her room... There's no more butter, no soap, no oil, no more rice. And no toilet paper...

MADO: How many for dinner?

AZAF: The group of American tourists and the Belgians. The Americans said they'd file a complaint when they got back home. They've never wiped themselves with banana leaves before. They say it gives them a rash.

MADO: Didn't they want a taste of the exotic? What are they complaining about? The rain stopped yesterday...

AZAF: What should we give them for dinner?

MADO: We'll deal with that. Don't worry. We'll tell them there's a surprise this evening, an exotic treat. We'll ground up the week leftovers with some hot peppers. And I'm seeing Zugrako later. He'll get us something.

AZAF: That pig.

MADO: Mind your own business. The kitchen stinks. I want everything to be spotless tonight, you hear.

AZAF: Then get rid of Makuma. She cries all the time, snivels and spits in the soup. The clients are going to notice at some point.

1

MADO: I can't fire her. She's my best work horse. She'll get over it.

AZAF: You know very well she won't.

MADO: She knew my terms. She accepted. Just drop the subject.

AZAF: Oh, and... there's no more milk in town. Not even for the babies at the orphanage. You might ask Zugrako this evening. Since he's supplying the hotel with stolen merchandise.

MADO: Shut up. Good thing the devil has given me the wits to keep this dump going and feed all you lazy bastards.

AZAF: (*He breaks the glass he is wiping.*) Bitch.

MADO: What did you say?

AZAF: Will you need me tonight?

MADO: You'll see.

AZAF: My mother is sick. I promised to go to the village to see her.

MADO: Your mother... (*She laughs.*) Careful now. Don't make fun of me. The prison's right across the street.

AZAF: She could come sleep here. I can't leave her alone.

MADO: Well, what are nursing homes for? I saw your mother the other day. She was carrying a full calabash on her head, tripping along like a young gazelle. Was it with my money you bought her that bubu brocade with flamboyant flowers? Come on, you filthy little cheat.

 Pause. Music and a nostalgic song waft in.

MADO: That's old Razu again. Tell him to go away. He scares the guests. How did he ever get to be so thin?

AZAF: He comes from the other side of the river. Where they're killing all the cattle because of the famine. He used to have his own herd.

MADO: Give him a dish of lentils. And ask him to polish the dance floor for tomorrow night. What a gorgeous day finally... after all that rain. Bring a deck chair to the terrace. *(She goes to the terrace and gazes out over the landscape. To herself)* Who remembers me now? You'll never leave me. Pierre... Pierre... "Drifting in the clouds I'll carry you across the world. You'll never leave me. I'm coming with you into the cold of the night. I turn around the earth, your body next to mine. It warms me. It burns me. I'll take you with me into the cold of the night." *(She laughs.)* I wrote you that... a long time ago. You remember? After we split up, when you left with her... How you must have laughed. Not as much as I do today... not as much as me.

Azaf comes out with a notebook.

MADO: So, come here... Let's see the inventory.

AZAF: This will be quick: Three boxes of crackers. Five bars of chocolate. A dozen cans of tomato sauce. Twelve pounds of lentils. Eight bottles of Pernod. Twenty kilos of manioc. And...

MADO: Rotten government... The same old story. It sucks. Too many restrictions to make any money here, so capital gets the hell out. Anyway, you'll always have your coconuts and your African sun to feed you lazy bastards. You're lucky. Take these orders to the kitchen. Tell them to prepare a feast for our beloved patron, our dearest tyrant Zugrako. A duck stuffed with mangos... and a pâté of game meat. Don't forget to put a bottle of champagne on ice and...

AZAF: The help will be happy. A real meal at last.

MADO: We'll keep the leftovers for the tourists. And tell Makuma to iron my red silk dress.

Azaf exits.
Mado starts to whistle. A bird replies.

MADO: Who remembers... who remembers me now... (*Mado whistles. The bird whistles.*) You are free. I'm stuck in this dump. So far... far from her... I've got enough money to leave... Why stay, huh? Why stay? All those houses I could buy, waiting for me in Geneva, Monte Carlo, Boston... All that gold stashed away... surrounding me like a fortress, protecting me from their hate. But who remembers... who remembers me now? The property, the money, all for her. If I could just see her. Then die. Here, take it all, my love. Please, it's for you. I want to hug you, to kiss you. I can't go on. Everything's rotten, burned. A horrible struggle... Corpses everywhere... vanished in the dust of time. I am walking in the desert... Stones... brown, purple, red... I can build with these... Take it all my love... My houses in Geneva, Rio, Grenada, Florence, all for you. Just to see you and then die. Die... What's wrong with me? It must be the sun after all these months of rain. I can live for another hundred years. (*She stretches out her arms.*) I want to live for another century. I could live off of everything I own, everything I can still get from these gutless bastards. (*She hums the "Goëland" melody by Damia*.*) You're not around to hear me, Pierre... but I can still sing. And drink to your health. (*Laughing*) "To your health, you shit." (*Shouting*) Azaf... Azaf! Bring me a gin and tonic.

Azaf rushes in with a tray.

MADO: (*She drinks and then gives Azaf a glass.*) Drink to my health, sweetheart. You know Zugrako is jealous of you. He should be... You are handsome, intelligent. He often warns me, don't forget the guy's a thief, one day he'll strangle you and steal your money... (*She laughs.*) That would be risky, wouldn't it, Azaf? And you love your Mado too, don't you? Say you love me. (*She takes his hand.*)

AZAF: (*Slowly sipping his drink, he withdraws his hand.*) My hands

---

* A 1930s hit song, made popular by Damia, a famous singer of the period.

are dirty. They stink. Smell them... I squashed hundreds of cockroaches. I have to get back to the kitchen. Clean everything. Scrub the floor. Polish the silver. Shine the crystal.

Gwen appears carrying a sketchbook.

MADO: Come and have a drink with us. Azaf, get a glass for our guest.

GWEN: No, thank you, I'm not thirsty.

MADO: You didn't go on the trip with the others?

Azaf exits.

GWEN: No. I heard the road to the volcano was flooded. And this sun... today... it makes me dizzy. I decided I'd rather go to the village and do some sketches.

MADO: Show me. (*Looking at the sketchbook*) What is it? Men carrying something... a stretcher... bottles... some standing, some spilled over... some drifting away.

GWEN: It's a funeral. A young boy, there on the stretcher, under the blanket... and the crowd following.

MADO: Oh yes, that was yesterday. It's Chalouf's son. Eight kids, the father crippled and this boy blind. Death was a blessing. He would have spent his life begging for the family. You have a lot of imagination. But you should draw happier things. Like me, basking in the sun on this terrace... Quite a view from here, don't you think?

GWEN: Yes. Paradise lost, and all these birds singing in the traveler's tree.

MADO: They're called *souis mangas*. They always sing when evening falls.

A short pause while the two women listen to the birds. Then a silence.

GWEN: It's getting dark.

MADO: Yes. Wouldn't you like to do my portrait?

GWEN: I'm sorry. I'm leaving tomorrow.

MADO: Why so soon?

GWEN: And I don't really know you well enough.

MADO: I'll give you a thousand dollars. You could stay a few more days. Really, I'd be delighted.

GWEN: I have to leave. But if you give me all your time until tomorrow, maybe...

MADO: All my time... Are you crazy? With all the work running this hotel, I don't have a minute to myself. I don't know what got into me... laying around like I had nothing to do. I must be tired. It's the sun after all those months of rain. The heat, the light... Did you notice? Last night the cactus flowers opened in the moonlight. Like white stars on giant candelabras... It's idiotic but... they remind me of... they remind me of snow... back in my country... and the first edelweiss. I was born in the Alps.

GWEN: You're Swiss?

MADO: Racing with Papa down the mountain. He'd let me ski along for a while, then all of a sudden he'd fly ahead of me... Just the time to cry out "Don't leave me behind, don't leave me," and he was gone, flying into the sun. So far, so very far away... So, what about this portrait? I'll give you a thousand bucks... Do as you please.

GWEN: It's hard.

MADO: Why?

GWEN: You're so different. Your face as a child in the snow and your face now...

MADO: (*laughing*) Stuck in the ice, huh? I'm not to your liking? Yet men find me beautiful. More beautiful at fifty, with all my experience and all my money, than I was at sixteen. (*She stretches.*) And I've never felt better. Do the portrait. I want it. And I feel comfortable with you, like I was with... What are you doing all alone in Africa?

GWEN: Money... You talk about your money all the time. Do you ever give any away?

MADO: Didn't I make you an offer?

> *A child's crying is heard. Makuma enters dragging a little girl with her.*

MAKUMA: She doesn't want to come in. She's afraid. Come on, Madame Mado will give you something to eat.

MADO: What now? I really don't have time. Take her away.

MAKUMA: Her name is Nesilili. Her grandmother just died. Tomorrow I'll take her to the orphanage.

MADO: That's Africa. You want to enjoy the sun, to fly off, but all the shit holds you to the ground. You can't expect me to feed the whole damn planet.

> *The little girl moves shyly toward Mado. She holds out her hand, attracted by the necklace the woman is wearing. It is a gold chain with a cross of rubies.*

MADO: You have good taste, little black fly. I never wear it, but today's a special occasion... His birthday and he's the one who... I never wear it. It stays locked in the safe with the gold and the jewelry. No use tempting the devil, huh? They'd strangle me and steal it off my body. They'd get caught and they know it. But they're so stupid. You can't trust them, you know. When hunger is the strongest. They'll rip off your head for a little gold. They get caught, they're beaten, they're kicked bloody and locked up. The prison is across the street. Still they believe, they hope that hunger will give them wings to get away... trade the chain and the cross for a little meat. Some rice. A woman for the night.

> *She takes off the necklace and hands it to Nesilili. The child stares at her in wide–eyed terror.*

MADO: Take it... Look how pretty it is... Do you like it? (*Nesilili grabs the necklace and puts the ruby cross in her mouth.*) Taste good? Yeah, suck on it... suck. For once maybe He didn't die in vain. (*She laughs.*) This is my blood, this is my flesh. Do you go to catechism, little girl?

GWEN: Nesilili, come here. Come, don't be afraid. You can sleep with me tonight. I have a big bed. And tomorrow...

MADO: What are you going to do with her tomorrow? (*To the girl*) Nesilili, do you want to go with the lady?

> *Frightened, Nesilili rushes to Makuma's arms.*

MADO: You see... Don't be afraid. Makuma will put a mat in the laundry room and tomorrow Azaf will take you to the orphanage... You'll be fine there. (*The child begins to wail.*) You'll have lots of little brothers and sisters there.

GWEN: (*to Makuma*) Can't you keep her with you? I'll give you money.

> *Makuma lowers her gaze and says nothing. The little girl clings to her more tightly.*

MAKUMA: Ask Madame... Really I can't. I am sick. Even my own child... my son... (*She cannot continue.*)

MADO: (*with sudden violence*) What's got into you, sniveling like that? And you, with your nose in your sketchbook, what are you drawing now? Don't you see anything? Don't you hear? These people don't even have enough to feed themselves, let alone take in another stray. The girl will be fine at the orphanage. Better than groveling in the mud, grubbing from trash bins.

GWEN: Is the orphanage that house surrounded by a big wall on the way to Derfu?

MAKUMA: Yes.

GWEN: It's so quiet. No shouts, no laughter. Are there a lot of them?

MAKUMA: Around sixty. Some come from the other side of the river. They're good children. Very good, very quiet. They sit in a circle or lie on the ground. They are waiting for their mother to come back.

MADO: Two remarkable women are looking after them.

MAKUMA: Yes, but they only have two arms. Oh, Madame, who is holding them? Who is rocking them to sleep?

MADO: Who is rocking them? Who will hold their hand when they come knocking in search of work or a piece of land and the door is slammed in their face? Better they learn from the start that they're abandoned.

GWEN: Do they ever go back to their village?

MAKUMA: No. The smarter ones leave the country. Others spend their life in prison. They learn to steal...

MADO: I had one working in the kitchen. This half–wit locked himself in the safe. He screamed for three solid hours until the police came.

MAKUMA: I'm going to cook some porridge for her. Come Nesilili, come with me.

She leaves with the girl.

GWEN: (*staring at Mado*) You seem tired. It's funny, you look like Rayre...

MADO: Who's Rayre?

GWEN: She's a bag lady who sleeps in the subway during the winter. In the summer she moves to Notre Dame square. She talks to the pigeons that nest in her hair. She calls them Ruby, Pearl, Topaz, Emerald, Saphire... in memory of her past fortune.

MADO: Me, a bag lady? You must be out of your mind. (*She laughs.*) I keep my money safely hidden away. No foolhardy expenses. (*A pause.*) I don't think you'll be able to leave tomorrow. I just heard the airport is closed. They're afraid of riots. Have you ever heard of Mori Salem? The verdict was today. It's night now. I wouldn't go to the village if I were you. Safer to stay in your room. Foreigners like you... it looks fishy, traveling all alone. You're watched.

GWEN: I am not alone. I have friends everywhere. Have a good evening. (*She exits.*)

MADO: (*smoothing her face*) Why get so upset? It's bad for my blood pressure, my heart. I'm in a sweat. It's my blood. All this blood imprisoned and beating, beating at me. This sweat streaming over me. Blood beating in my head. My belly. My legs. My legs feel so heavy. I won't be able to dance with him tonight. (*She massages her legs.*) "You seem tired..." A bag lady. Little bitch. You'll pay for this. She's right. I am tired. The sun... the first edelweiss... I mean the cactus flowers. Ah, to run in the snow. I should leave, get the hell out of here. They surround me, smiling politely with clenched fists behind their backs. One day they'll kill me. I like the danger, provoking them. But they wouldn't dare. Who's going to give them work? Who's going to feed them? (*A laugh*) But sister, you'll get yours, just wait.

She goes to the phone and dials.

Hello... Colonel Zugrako, please... Hello, darling...Yes, tonight. I'm preparing a feast fit for a king. Everything you like... Of course I'll be beautiful... Yes... Yes... I thought so... No... A letter? Yes, Azaf found it in her room. She wants to see Mori Salem... He's going to be executed?... Tomorrow... Fine. I'll watch her. She says she has to leave tomorrow, but... Lock her in the room? That's not easy. Send two policemen over for the night... Okay... Yes, my honey bear, see you then.

Old Razu's drum is heard again.

SCENE 2

Evening.

In Gwen's room.

Gwen is packing. She picks up a book and searches for the letter which has disappeared. She goes to the door. It is locked. She goes to the window and is about to climb out, but Azaf enters from the window and pushes her back into the room.

AZAF: I'm sorry, but I'm just doing my job. My orders are to keep you in your room. (*He exits through the window and locks an iron bar in place.*)

In Mado's room.

Makuma is helping Mado dress.

MADO: I'm getting fat. I'm going on a diet tomorrow. No more liquor. No more pastry. It's ridiculous, but all these people starving make me hungry. All these funerals call for champagne, don't you think? Did you get a drink in the kitchen? For God's sake, stop sniveling, stop it. (*Gwen's beating her fists on the wall is heard.*) Do you hear that? Thank God the tourists haven't come back from their excursion. Keep trying to knock down the wall, beating your head against the wall, that's all you can do... Little bitch. I know this type, always judging you. Saying nothing, but condemning you, provoking you with their smug faces. When time comes to say something, to do something, they're lost in their dreams. That letter... she must be incredibly stupid to have hidden it in her room.

MAKUMA: She is always alone. There are a lot of books in her room, and drawings. She talked to me. She asked me what I did after work, if I had a husband...

MADO: She couldn't run a hotel in this shit hole. Stuck in the bush. Nothing but the smell of crushed cockroaches and droopy palm trees. Who opened a nightclub here, a swimming pool, a game room, where the tourists spend all their money? Certainly not you crummy bunch of... (*Makuma tightens Mado's belt.*) Ouch, you're hurting me. Would you stop crying? And that whipped–dog face, it's depressing. Did you go to the orphanage to see your son today?

MAKUMA: No. They won't let me in unless I have a health certificate.

MADO: Go to the clinic.

MAKUMA: At the clinic they ask for a paper from you. Mado Forgus declares that Makuma Nyagon works for me and is in good health...

MADO: You know I can't do that. You're sick.

MAKUMA: How can this stop me from kissing my son? It's not right. And I'm not sick. How could I work as hard as I do if I were sick? (*Laughing*) Yesterday I even dug the big hole on the river bank for the garbage. Do you know what I found digging? A golden picture frame. The photo was gone. Can I keep the frame to put a picture of my son?

MADO: A golden frame?

MAKUMA: The director of the orphanage gave me the photo. The day he went in, for his identity card. (*She pulls out a photograph from her pocket.*) See. Djena Nyagon, number 107 MX 12... How he stares at me. "Why did you leave me here... why?" It looks like he'll never smile again. Open eyes waiting... every night. Wondering will my mother come? Madame, if you agree, I can still get him back. The director said three months. You have three months to reclaim him. After that...

MADO: (*brushing her hair*) What's gotten into you today? First the little runt, now your son. I don't want any kids around here. I told you that. You're free to leave if you want.

MAKUMA: But Madame, where can I go without a health certificate?

MADO: Then stay, but stop sniveling. You can have a dozen later. If you hadn't been so stupid you wouldn't be in this state. Did you ever stop to think "How will I pay the doctor, how will I feed the child?" No, you just thought about having fun and parading your big belly in the sun.

MAKUMA: He's waiting for me. I know. Every night. Every night I rock him and sing to him. Do you think he can hear me?

Makuma sings a lullaby as she straightens up the room.

MADO: Don't be ridiculous. Just leave that for now. Go get some rest before dinner. (*In spite of herself, Mado begins chanting something like a nursery rhyme under her breath.*)

> *Little girl in a meadow*
> *Chased by the sun*
> *Little girl in a meadow*
> *Jumps in the rapids*
> *Chased by the sun*
> *And swims, pushed by the wind,*
> *Chased by the sun.*

MAKUMA: You never talk about your daughter.

MADO: No children, no regrets.

Gwen is again beating on the wall.

MADO: The first time she opened her eyes it was to judge me. Condemn me... Tell Azaf to shut her up.

The song of old Razu is heard.

In Gwen's room.

Gwen is lying on the bed. Azaf enters with a bowl of fruit.

AZAF: Eat something. You'll feel better.

GWEN: I'm suffocating. Open the window.

He unlocks the iron bar. She goes to the window.

AZAF: It's of no use. She's stronger than we are. She'll always be stronger.

GWEN: Do you know this Mori Salem?

AZAF: Yes. He's a very generous man. But he couldn't do anything for us. He tried. He failed.

GWEN: (*She cuts a mango in two.*) Here, have some.

They eat in silence.

GWEN: You're a strange kind of servant.

AZAF: Servant?

GWEN: Yes, you know, someone who takes orders.

AZAF: I'm well fed. (*Laughing, he smacks his belly.*) Look at my stomach. You've seen how thin people are here. So thin... just skin and bones. Imagine making love when you're just a pack of bones, imagine rolling in the sand like that. You'd get bruises all over. No, you need good food. She gives me everything I want.

GWEN: She has no right to keep that letter. How can she refuse I take a message to a condemned man?

AZAF: Tomorrow he'll be executed.

GWEN: You must know the prison guards. How can I get in?

AZAF: It's too dangerous. Don't get involved in that stuff. Be like the others. Look at the palm trees, listen to the wind singing through the branches, get a good tan under our African sun, take a few pictures for later, when you're old...

GWEN: I know I'm a foreigner, but this man trusted me. Do you understand that, Azaf? Why did he give me the letter at the airport? Tomorrow Mori Salem will be hung. I have to bring him the letter... Let me go.

AZAF: I can't. Just calm down. Try to sleep. (*He fans her gently.*) Close your eyes... sleep... sweet dreams. Who knows where you'll be tomorrow? Maybe in that prison across the street.

GWEN: Tell Mado I need to see her. I can persuade her. I know how. Please...

AZAF: She won't come. In an hour Zugrako will be here for dinner. She's taking her bath. Putting on perfume. Slipping on her loveliest dress. She's afraid of him. Then she'll go by the kitchen to put some spices in the wine... some herbs in the sauce. She'll check to see if the tablecloth is spotless, the crystal sparkling... It's going to be a beautiful night. If she doesn't need me, I'll come back and visit. I'll tell you the story of the star that rises after all the others, right over the traveler's tree...

GWEN: Tell her I'm sick, Azaf. Go get her.

AZAF: She won't come. She can't stand any trouble before a good meal and a night of love. Your forehead is burning. You have a fever. Wait. I'll get you a cool cloth. Maybe things will work out for you, who knows. It's too late for me. You're right. I'm like her slave. But I don't have the guts to go out and beg or join the army. (*He puts a cool cloth on her forehead.*) Are you feeling any better?

GWEN: Yes, much better, thank you. Thank you very much.

AZAF: I liked this guy, Mori Salem. He thinks our land is rich enough to feed everybody, that we just need to share. But he's a madman. How can he say that? What belongs to you, belongs to you. If you're thirsty, you're not going to share your jug. If you're afraid of going hungry, you won't give up your cow.

GWEN: Some people store gold in safes.

AZAF: They'll tell you it's their work and their due, their wealth belongs to them. And all the others are just lazy. These bums should be grateful to them, because if it weren't for the rich, the poor would die even sooner. You're an artist. I saw your drawings when I was looking for the letter. Your drawings talk, they tell me things I couldn't imagine just looking with everyday eyes. Our eyes get worn out looking at things. You give us new eyes, eyes that wake up in the morning sun. (*He caresses her face.*) God has given everyone their own burden.

GWEN: Look how my hands are shaking. I can't even draw anymore. Let me leave. I'll be happy to be out of this country. Do you see that? In the tree there...

AZAF: You mean the weaverbirds?

GWEN: No, I see children's faces. They're falling from the branches. There, another one falls. Another. Then silence. Nothing moves. Look! Their heads are crushed like rotten fruit and blood is flowing from their mouths. Don't you see?

AZAF: Quiet down. You have a high fever. Quiet now.

GWEN: Can't you see all the cut hands waving from the branches... begging for help? It's too late. I can do nothing. Let me get up. (*Moving to the window*) The hands are caught in the branches. The wind has pushed their faces into the dirt. The tree is silent. Where did the birds go?

AZAF: You'll be alright. It's just the African sun. Then this moon. After all that rain. Rest now. I'll get you something to drink.

SCENE 3

Night.
On the terrace of the Artistic Hotel.

Zugrako and Mado clink glasses in a toast.
A song in German drifts from one of the hotel rooms.

MADO: They killed three gazelles and an antelope... They'll get drunk and fall asleep... The animals are lucky. The privilege of killing them costs a lot.

ZUGRAKO: Are you sure she can't run away?

MADO: Yes. Azaf is watching her and I took her passport.

ZUGRAKO: My men will come to get her in the morning. Tonight they're all busy guarding the prison. Mori Salem's people might try to free him. Can you trust Azaf?

MADO: Yes. I paid off a judge for his release. He knows he'll never find work anyplace else.

ZUGRAKO: (*He kisses her.*) You are terrific... You scare me... The day I'm down, you'll be the first to spit in my face, won't you?

MADO: (*She caresses him.*) Without you I'd be lost... When I came here I found this filthy place. The Artistic Hotel, that's what the former owner named it. He was an artist and a drunk. He painted snowy landscapes all over the walls. They were covered with blood stains, squashed mosquitoes, vomit, rotting cockroaches... A dirty little hotel like so many others in Africa... Nights of suffocating heat, all the fans broken. And days when you want to put a gun in your mouth...

ZUGRAKO: And now... a swimming pool, a game room, a nightclub... Tennis courts, a golf course. What else could you ask for, my lovely Mado?

MADO: Grub. We can't let the tourists starve, can we? What can you get us?

ZUGRAKO: Soap. Butter. Oil. Corned beef and sardines. Canned milk.

MADO: Canned milk?

ZUGRAKO: Yeah, a whole shipment for the orphanage that my men confiscated at the airport.

MADO: Makuma will make luscious vanilla puddings for you, honey bear.

ZUGRAKO: Just sell what's left over on the black market and we'll split the profit. My philosophy is close one eye and keep the other on your pocket. If you don't make a profit, the next guy will. The director of the orphanage will be happy to find milk for his kids, thanks to us.

MADO: Of course... You must be a very rich man, Zugrako.

ZUGRAKO: Not really. I have to grease a lot of palms to stay on top. And my sons studying in Geneva, that costs a bundle. Then this sorcerer told me I'd die of prostate cancer. So I'm putting money aside for an operation in Switzerland, a place on Lake Léman... You never know. But what about you? What do you do with your money? You don't have any family... and your honey bear takes care of you, right?

Azaf brings in a dish full of meat.

MADO: Taste this. Close your eyes and let it melt in your mouth.

ZUGRAKO: (*He chews slowly.*) It's good... very good... Fresh meat roasted in the sun... fit for a king... A buck killed and quartered on the spot, basted in his own blood... Such flavor... It gives me a hard on.

MADO: Azaf.

AZAF: Madame?

MADO: Bring Gwen here.

AZAF: Suppose she refuses to come.

MADO: Drag her here.

ZUGRAKO: What's got into you? You're the only one I want in my bed tonight.

MADO: You're getting old. A little spice won't hurt. (*To Azaf*) Tell her to put on her best dress, tell her Mado Forgus is giving a party tonight. (*Azaf exits. Mado stretches and stands.*) Let's dance. I need to digest. (*They dance, locked together in a tender embrace.*) Faster... faster... Let's take off... fly away together... Let's explode. (*She fondles his buttocks.*) All that fat to burn off... all the fat of our full bellies lights one hell of a fire below, doesn't it my love? Hold me closer.

ZUGRAKO: Just us two. The whole world is ours. We'll swallow it, digest it, shit it out. And we'll always be hungry.

MADO: (*laughing*) We're condemned to one perpetual orgasm. Who's going to feel sorry for us?

ZUGRAKO: Aren't you scared?

MADO: Why should I be? Who remembers me? I'm alone forever. I want to die coming, and you're here, my honey bear.

ZUGRAKO: Whatever made you so greedy?

MADO: And you so cruel?

> *Gwen enters dressed in black.*
> *Mado rushes over to her.*

MADO: Please forgive me. Let's have some fun. Come dance with me.

Gwen stands totally immobile.

MADO: Are you mad at me? Let's forgive and forget. We're very different, but we're really very close, aren't we? I have the feeling I know you... that I've seen you... over there. This is Colonel Zugrako, a friend. Gwen, you should have brought your sketches. Zugrako here likes art. Actually he's an artist himself. He sings and dances and collects fire arms.

ZUGRAKO: Quite unique pieces from all over the world. Come, have a drink with us. (*Raising his glass*) To the health of all artists, and to our hostess, the owner of the Artistic Hotel, to the incomparable Mado Forgus.

GWEN: I don't drink. (*Pause.*) Where are your policemen?

ZUGRAKO: What policemen? Ah, that business with the letter. We'll fix that tomorrow. Just a few questions, an identity check. Don't worry about it. Let the African night work its magic. It's full of mystery, perfumes. Come dance with us. We'll see to that tomorrow.

MADO: You're pale. Eat some meat. It's a buck cooked in its own blood, baked in the sun, with herbs of the savanna. You need to get your strength back.

GWEN: Why? For the interrogation?

MADO: My dear, to live! If you just trust me, in a few days this evening will be a pleasant memory. Zugrako... (*She takes a letter from her pocket and burns it over the candle flame.*) I'm burning this letter. We'll never speak of it again. Gwen, you never even heard of Mori Salem. Tomorrow you'll go back to Paris. And now let's drink to this ghost...

GWEN: (*raising an empty glass*) Let's drink to the health of Mori

Salem. Zugrako, perhaps you could explain what the letter means. I didn't really understand, although I learned it by heart: "In the savanna take the first trail leading to the baobab, dig a hole, empty the calabash and make a mask with the mud. Make it so hard that even the lion's claws can't tear it. Take the second trail leading to the volcano and make a shield with the lava. Make it so hard that even the vulture's beak can't pierce it. Then take the third trail through the cave that leads to the Bayakevit forest. Wash in the brook, eat from the fig tree, and you will be ready to meet the fiercest of your enemies."

MADO: (*She bursts out laughing.*) That's the last message to Mori Salem? A poem, a parable? You would have done better to bring him an arm to kill his guard. But that's how you are, you artists; you prefer words... Christ, it sounds like the Bible. The last shall be first. Happy are the poor for they shall inherit the kingdom of heaven... What a great idea, huh, honey bear? Artists! Weeping with one eye about the world's misery, blinking in the sun with the other, admiring the beauty of nature...

ZUGRAKO: I drank too much wine. I need to piss and get comfortable. (*He puts his arms around both women's shoulders.*) We're friends, aren't we?... I think I ate too much.

> *He exits, lurching.*
> *Gwen pulls out a bundle of letters and torn checks which she scatters on the floor.*

GWEN: (*in a low voice*) She told me when you see her, tell her to leave me alone. "In any case I'm leaving France, she'll never find me." So... these are your letters she never opened... your checks she never cashed. "I'm leaving France, I'll never see her again... She should lock her money away in her heart. It's a safe nobody can get into. All I want is never to see her again."

MADO: (*in a whisper*) Where did you meet her?

GWEN: In a train. I liked her right away. She has the face of a child who knows a secret. I told her of my plans to go to Africa, a blind escape, never to come back. She understood. Staring out the window—it was raining—she said "I'd come with you, but I made a promise." She said she knew someone in Timenime... a woman who runs a hotel... the Artistic Hotel.

MADO: (*slowly picking up the letters*) But why... why? Was she dressed warmly? She was always running out without even a sweater on. I knitted her a big white wool sweater, with gold clasps and little flowers on the collar. She didn't want to wear it. Ever. How is she? Has she put on some weight? Does she eat enough? That's all she said? "All I want is never to see her again." She still loves me. Nothing can separate us. Not even her absence... especially not her absence.

GWEN: She gave me this for you.

Gwen gives Mado a mirror.

MADO: (*She gazes into the mirror and then throws it down.*) It's the wine that makes my eyes swollen. I'm hot. I'm sweating. It's pouring down my arm pits, my back... running down my thighs. (*She wipes herself with her dress.*) It's okay. Just high blood pressure... the wine... the meat, raw, marinated in the sun... strong meat, heavy spices... She couldn't keep that baby. It would have killed her. She was so young, so frail. The doctor told me she couldn't, it would have been madness, insane to keep this fetus, this shit which would blow her up, kill her. I told her... again and again... she wasn't capable of the suffering... screaming hours in labor... raising a child.... Where would she find the money, huh? How would she raise it? She didn't know how to do anything. And the kid would have taken after that no good son of a bitch who...

GWEN: Will you help me? For the sake of her memory? I have to see Mori Salem before they hang him.

MADO: She tricked you. I can't do anything for you. Sure, you can see Mori Salem. They'll lock you up in a cell next to his. You'll be in the same prison. Why did you come here? Why, huh?

(*She moves toward Gwen.*) I could ring your neck... Filthy little liar. Is that all you can come up with? My daughter? I don't give a shit. (*She spits in Gwen's face.*)

GWEN: (*wiping her face slowly*) I have your portrait to finish.

MADO: You're nuts. But why not? Paint me the way I was at sixteen. When I was the prettiest, when I thought to love was to hold, that as long as I loved them, no one would ever leave me. Paint my picture by tomorrow and you'll be released. You have my word.

> *Zugrako enters holding Azaf by the collar.*

ZUGRAKO: Come on... Join the party... Let's dance. We're all friends here, aren't we?

> *Azaf wrenches himself free with such force that Zugrako almost falls.*

ZUGRAKO: Boy, I will have your hide. You want to know when? Maybe tomorrow. But we have all night to dance.

> *Zugrako has removed his bubu and stands barechested. He wears a necklace and has wrapped a broadcloth around his hips.*

ZUGRAKO: This is the way the tourists like to see us. It really gives them a charge, the groupies, the hard boiled eggs, the milk curds, the toothless hens and the bald roosters singing cockle–doodle–do to the coconut trees... Blue–eyed pigs...

> *Thoroughly drunk Zugrako dances alone to the distant sound of Razu's tam tam.*

MADO: You're wrong about her, honey bear–rh–rrh (*She growls, then howls like a hyena.*) She is not the dancing type. She's the kind who'll put a bullet in your head to free the slaves. No, no, that's not it. She is an artist. She'll just take her crayons and go quietly draw in the corner. (*She laughs.*) How will you paint me? In a white dress, with a flower in my hair?

ZUGRAKO: (*still dancing*) What slaves? There are no more slaves...
Everybody's free... free to kill. No more slaves, just corpses.
(*Roaring*) Blood, I love blood. (*He sweeps Gwen in his arms and
forces her to dance.*) Come, my beauty, you might as well enjoy
your last night.

> *The drums stop. They continue dancing in silence.*
> *Mado takes a hefty drink. Azaf lies down at her feet. Mado begins*
> *to vomit.*

MADO: I drank too much. Keep dancing... don't mind me. It's nothing. I need another drink. (*She nudges Azaf with her foot, as if he
were a dog.*) Get up. Go fetch Makuma. I've soiled my dress. Tell
her to bring me my engagement gown. The only one I brought
with me. And get the paint box from the room of this bitch.

> *Azaf exits.*
> *Mado lurches over to Gwen.*

MADO: I want you to do my portrait now. Look at me. The way
I am. Drunk and covered with vomit, full of hate. Do you hear
me? And if I don't like it, I'll tell Zugrako to break your little
wrists, crush your little fingers. Ah, you wanted to paint me as
I was... the most beautiful, the most beloved... I didn't want
this child. I did everything I could to get rid of it. But she hung
on. She came into the world judging me, condemning me. At
fifteen she was taunting me and to really screw me up she went
and got pregnant with that no good son of a bitch... And she
whined and cried, "Please, Mama, let me keep it... I'll stay in
school, I'll work at night, the doctor told me I could never have
another one." The stupid little bitch. (*She tears off her dress.*)
Makuma... Makuma!

> *Makuma enters with Gwen's paint box and a dress which must*
> *have been splendid, but is now faded and tattered. She takes*
> *Mado—sunk to the floor and curled in a ball—into her arms*
> *and begins to rock her like a baby.*

MAKUMA: There, there... Hush, now... (*She sings a lullaby.*)

Gwen picks up her brushes and begins to paint the portrait while Makuma sings.
Mado stands and Makuma dresses her in the engagement gown.
Stiffly, Mado walks over to the bar and pours another drink. Then she walks straight to Zugrako.

MADO: Get out, you vulture. I need to be alone.

ZUGRAKO: What's gotten into you? You reek of wine. Let's just go to bed.

MAKUMA: *(to Mado)* You're shaking. Do you want your shawl? The night is getting cold. Let me take you to bed. Come with me.

ZUGRAKO: It's the wine that's making you sentimental. Sentimentality makes me vomit. To hell with sentimentality... Let's drink to that... To hell with... sentiment... I've had too much to drink too. Please forgive me, lovely monster. Tomorrow everything will start over... interrogation, torture, verdict, execution... torture, interrogation, verdict, execution... All I want now is to have a good time. Get in shape to enjoy the screams, the insults, the blood. You're the only one strong enough to help me out of this rut. And you know very well you need me. Without me you'd be nothing, just a pile of slimy rags. I could close this hotel on the spot and you'd be naked like the first day you came. Do you remember? *(He draws her in his arms.)* You were so skinny and hunched over. *(He laughs.)* I've made you into a goddess.

MADO: *(yielding to his embrace)* My honey bear, how could I forget? I don't know what came over me. The cactus flowers blooming last night... the snow, the first edelweiss... Papa flying into the sun on his skis. Don't leave me, please, don't leave me alone. *(She caresses his face.)* You can't really understand... the snow... the first flakes falling. I used to catch them on my tongue. He'd warm my frozen feet in his hands. Hug me. Keep me warm.

ZUGRAKO: Come, it's time for bed. Azaf, keep an eye on the lady.

MAKUMA: Madame, tomorrow is the last day I can get my son from the orphanage. Please, Madame Mado, let suffering soften your heart. I beg you, I want to keep the boy here with me. Outside we'll die of hunger. You can protect us. I'll work all day, all night. I will never leave you. I will love you like the banana tree loves the sun. Please... listen to me.

> *Makuma kisses Mado's hands and pursues her as she exits under Zugrako's arm.*
> *Old Razu's nostalgic song is heard.*
> *Feverishly, Gwen is working on her portrait.*
> *Azaf is cleaning food, broken glass, and vomit from the floor.*

AZAF: You should get some sleep. This portrait is just one of her whims.

GWEN: It's my revenge.

AZAF: (*He pours two glasses of wine and brings one to Gwen.*) This is our last night. Tomorrow Zugrako will skin us alive. We've seen too much.

GWEN: I can give you an address in France where you'll be safe, where you can work. There's an old woman who lives on the coast. She takes in all kinds of strays. The house is big. She would welcome you. Then, when you find friends, you can go someplace else. You won't be alone anymore. Azaf, do you understand what I'm saying?

AZAF: Yes, I'd like to do that. But I can't leave my country.

GWEN: The earth belongs to everybody. That's our country. Who told you this place where you can't live any longer is your country?

AZAF: My brother went to France, but he came back. He worked in a factory near Paris, *aux Lilas*, you know it? He loved the name "lilacs", but apparently the only flowers there were behind walls. He got homesick. He came back after seven years. He didn't even recognize home. His memories were all lies. He'd lost his memory . A man without a memory is like an infant born from a crocodile, floating along the river until he drifts to an unknown land. Abdu didn't understand us any more and we didn't understand him. He'd sit for hours in front of his hut listening to the birds. He asked me why he couldn't be like a bird, with the world as his country, nesting winters in the mango trees and summers in the elms. He died alone, walking out to the ocean. (*He moves toward Gwen.*) I don't know anything about you. We'll never see each other after tomorrow.

GWEN: We can still save Mori Salem. If we kill Zugrako. Then there would be riots and, with the help of his friends, Salem could escape.

AZAF: I don't want to die. Another Zugrako would move in and he might be even worse.

GWEN: No one will suspect you. Just look the other way while I run to the kitchen. Makuma will bring him his coffee tomorrow morning, like every day. It's quite simple.

AZAF: He's very suspicious.

GWEN: Don't worry.

> She takes a package of powder from her shoe and pours half into Azaf's hand. A pause.

AZAF: It's too dangerous for you. You don't know where Makuma hides the sugar. I'll go.

GWEN: (*kissing him*) You are brave. The two of us can do it, you'll see.

> Azaf exits. Gwen continues to paint.
> Makuma enters holding Nesilili by the hand.

MAKUMA: Nesilili can't sleep... (*She takes a plate from the table and begins to collect the leftover food.*) Famine on the other side of the river... The animals are dying one after another... These leftovers could feed people for a good month... Eat, Nesilili... eat whatever you want.

The little girl remains immobile, paralyzed with fear.

GWEN: Don't be afraid, Nesilili. Everybody's sleeping now. Do you like colors? (*She hands her the brush and easel. Hesitating, Nesilili begins to paint.*) Look, you can do this... that... Just let the brush go where it wants... There... that's it.

The child suddenly halts her painting and rushes to Makuma's arms.

MAKUMA: Azaf is taking her to the orphanage tomorrow. She knows that.

GWEN: Doesn't she have any family? A grandmother? An aunt who'd take care of her?

MAKUMA: No, nobody. (*She caresses the child.*) It's better for you, little gazelle. You're so pretty. They'll love you at the orphanage and you know, tourists come and visit. Sometimes they're touched and they take little girls like you back to their country. They are rich, a lot richer than us, and they'll give you good food. You'll become a big, strong girl. You'll get used to living far away. You're luckier than my son. His mother abandoned him, but she's alive. Nobody will take him. He'll spend his life at the orphanage. And me so close by... who can't even go to kiss him good night. They say I'm sick, but that's not true. (*Smiling through her tears, she lifts the child in the air and twirls her around.*) See how strong I am. I could take you far, far away... How far do you want to go, Nesilili?

The child laughs with delight.

GWEN: Makuma, you are so beautiful. Why do you stay here? You could find work someplace else.

Out of breath, Makuma stops. She sinks into a chair.

MAKUMA: You see. I got dizzy.

GWEN: I've seen how she looks at you. She needs you. You could fight back. Makuma, defend yourself.

MAKUMA: (*sadly*) It's true I'm sick. She keeps me. She could throw me out. I'd do anything for her. If I could just have my son back, I'd be healthy again, I know it. She's our only hope. Madame, please ask her.

GWEN: I have to finish this portrait. Who knows? It might touch her. (*Desperately painting, she murmurs to herself and Makuma.*) If I could just capture that look... You know when she talks about the snow and her father... Wait... "The first edelweiss... Papa flying into the sun... so far... so far away... the snow flakes on my tongue... my frozen feet in his hands..." Makuma, help me. Sing something. I can't do this alone. Please.

Makuma goes to Nesilili who has remained frozen like a statue. The woman wraps her arms around the girl's knees and sings.

MAKUMA:

> *Our mother who is in heaven,*
> *you have given birth in pain,*
> *to the sun*
> *and the earth*
> *the moon and the stars,*
> *give us this day our daily bread*
> *to all who are hungry,*
> *give us our bread with our daily sun,*
> *give us our bread that the stars of the night*
> *might light the eyes of all men.*
> *Our mother who is in heaven*
> *and on earth,*
> *give us the strength to give birth in pain*
> *to the fruit of our love...*

During the song the child remains rigid, her gaze filled with horror.
The light has shifted.
Gwen resumes her painting. Makuma lies down on the floor, clutching Nesilili in her arms.

SCENE 4

Dawn.
In the hotel lounge.

Mado is at the bar.
Makuma and Azaf are preparing to leave.

MAKUMA: The little girl doesn't want to be left alone. Somebody has to take care of her until we get back.

MADO: (*flat voice*) Are you sure the body's wedged in the bags of flour? Be careful. The road is very bad because of the floods. At every bend, the truck might spill the load. You know if they suspect us, we'll all be hung.

AZAF: Why not bury him under the garbage? The trip would be safer at night.

MAKUMA: What about the stench? He already smells bad.

MADO: Makuma, did you taste his coffee this morning?

MAKUMA: Yes, Madame.

MADO: Do you think he died of indigestion?

AZAF: Didn't you notice after dinner? How livid he was, his eyes glazed? Like he could see he was going to die.

MADO: Who's going to believe me? I was in my bath. He came toward me with his arms stretched out, his mouth wide open. I thought he wanted to hit me. And then he collapsed. He reeled back, his head struck the floor... not a word... his naked body...

MAKUMA: Azaf and I had a hard time carrying him to the truck. All that meat... The vultures will have a feast.

MADO: You'll each get a thousand dollars when you come back.

MAKUMA: A thousand dollars?

MADO: You'll sign a paper saying you were accomplices. I know it wasn't you, but if it ever got into your heads to talk.

MAKUMA: I don't want any money. I just want my son back. We'll go to the orphanage after I return... If you won't, I'll tell the truth. I don't care if they kill me.

MADO: (*She laughs.*) Is it Zugrako's death that's made you so brave?... I'm exhausted. Take advantage of the situation. Go get your son.

MAKUMA: Oh, thank you, Madame, thank you...

> *They exit.*
> *The tam tam and song of Old Razu are heard.*
> *Mado listens until the truck starts and pulls away.*
> *She exits and returns with a coat and a suitcase. She manipulates a door revealing the safe. She opens the safe and begins to stack gold bars into the suitcase.*
> *Gwen enters and does not see Mado behind the panel. She places the painting on the counter.*
> *Hearing a noise, Gwen goes to the wall, discovers Mado, and sees the gold bars gleaming inside the safe.*

GWEN: All this gold. What will you do with it?... Don't you want to see your portrait? I finished.

> *The portrait has two faces: one that of a child, the other a woman with a vicious look.*

MADO: (*She goes to the bar and pours a drink. Then she raises her glass to the painting.*) To your health, my dear... When I look like you, I'll need tons of gold to keep me warm and attract young men. (*To Gwen*) Tempting, isn't it? It's all mine. Mine, you hear? I worked my ass off, I slaved for this. Now I'm free and I'm getting the hell out of here with my money. I'll buy property in Paris, Geneva, San Francisco, Grenada. I can buy whatever I want. I can even buy off death. (*With sudden fury*) Even death, I'm stronger than death. I'll die when I choose. Standing up.

Shots and then the rumble of a mob are heard.

GWEN: They must be looking for Zugrako. They're surrounding the house.

MADO: Don't worry. With all my money, I can buy anything. Stay with me.

GWEN: No.

Nesilili runs in.

NESILILI: I'm scared... (*She clings to Gwen.*) I am scared. Don't let them take me. I don't want to go. Keep me with you.

GWEN: Why don't you leave with the little girl? I'll catch up with you later, I swear.

MADO: Are you nuts? I have all this stuff to carry.

GWEN: All right, then. (*She laughs and lifts Nesilili in the air.*) How light you are. You'll spur me along when I get tired... Come quickly. We're leaving.

She sticks a few gold bars in her bag.

GWEN: You've got plenty left. Buy the whole world if you want. Build yourself a golden tomb. By the way, Yvonne killed herself. She died alone at the hospital. She made me swear I would say nothing to you, whatever happened... Come, Nesilili, come... (*She picks up the girl.*) Yvonne's buried in an unmarked grave. Maybe you can buy her a tombstone when you get back to France.

She exits with Nesilili.

MADO: (*calling softly*) Yvonne... Yvonne...

> *She goes to the painting and caresses the face of the child.*
> *She starts to laugh.*
> *She puts the gold bars back into the safe, takes off her coat, goes*
> *to the telephone, and dials.*

MADO: Hello... I need to speak to the general... General? Zugrako has been assassinated... Oh, you've heard?... They're rioting... Mori Salem has escaped?... It's a young woman. She will try to leave the country. She has a little girl with her... No, the body is gone. Her accomplices took it to the Kumba forest to bury... Yes, they will be coming back... this evening... No. They suspect nothing... Good, I'll be expecting you then... Everything will be ready.

> *She puts on her jewelry. Then she picks up a gun and fires two*
> *shots into the portrait.*
> *The lights come down.*

~

ABLA FARHOUD

GAME OF PATIENCE

Translated from the French by

JILL MAC DOUGALL

UBU REPERTORY THEATER PUBLICATIONS
NEW YORK

Abla Farhoud was born in a small village in Lebanon . She emigrated to Canada in 1951. She has been acting professionally since the age of seventeen, and has appeared on Canadian television. In 1965, she returned to her native country where she lived for four years, pursuing her acting career. In 1969, she made a trip to Paris that resulted in a four-year stay. She studied theater at the University of Paris VIII and worked with director Jorge Lavelli. She returned to Quebec in 1973, gave birth to two children, and received her MFA in theater arts at the University of Quebec in Montreal. Her first play, *Quand j'étais grande,* was produced in 1983 in the third Festival de Création de Femmes. *Les Filles du 5 - 10 - 15¢,* published by Editions Lansman in Belgium, was premiered in 1986 at the Théâtre de Quat'sous in Montreal; it was subsequently produced in France, at the 1992 Festival International des Francophonies at Limoges, where she was invited as a resident writer; at the 1993 Avignon Festival, off; and at the Pavillon du Charolais in Paris (1993). Translated into English by Jill Mac Dougall, it was published by Ubu Repertory Theater in *Plays by Women: An International Anthology I* (1988) and given two public readings at Ubu. *Jeux de patience (Game of Patience)* was premiered at the Théâtre de la Licorne in Montreal in March, 1994. Abla Farhoud is the recipient of two French prizes: the 1993 Arletty Prize for her contribution to French-language theater and the "Théâtre et Liberté" Prize awarded by the French Société des Auteurs et Compositeurs Dramatiques (SACD) for her 1993 play, *La Possession du Prince.* Her other recent plays are: *La Camisole rouge* (1988), *Apatride* (1992-93) and *Shah contre Shah* (1993).

Jill Mac Dougall has been active in directing productions and conducting workshops, in translating plays, and in performance research in Europe, Africa and North America for over twenty years. Her translations for Ubu include *The Eye* (Bernard Zadi Zaourou), *The Girls from the 5 and 10* (Abla Farhoud), *Lost Voices* (Diur N'Tumb), *You Have Come Back* (Fatima Gallaire-Bourega), *Burn River Burn* (Jean–Pol Fargeau), *The Crossroads* (Josué Kossi Efoui) and *That Old Black Magic* (Koffi Kwahulé) all published in the series Ubu Repertory Theater Publications. She holds a Ph.D. in Performance Studies (NYU) and is presently teaching acting and theatre history with Pennsylvania State University.

The translation of *Game of Patience* was made possible by a grant from the National Theater Translation Fund.

Game of Patience, in Jill Mac Dougall's translation, had its first staged reading at Ubu Repertory Theater, 15 West 28th Street, New York, NY 10001, on May 9th, 1994.

TRANSLATOR'S NOTE

patience, n. 1. the bearing of provocation, annoyance, misfor-tune, pain, etc. without complaint, loss of temper, irritation or the like. 2. an ability or willingness to suppress restlessness or annoyance in waiting... 3. quiet perseverance; even–tempered care; diligence... 4. cards, solitaire...[1]

Consulting with the playwright, I have sought to make as clear as possible her vision of the theatrical space, the cultural idioms of the play, and the occasional Arabic terms of the dialogue. With American actors in mind, I have devised a transliteration system for these terms. Since transliteration is always arbitrary and can only approximate the music of the language, I strongly advise that the cast work with a pronunciation coach. All of these expressions are translated in the flow of the dialogue or in the end notes. I have also included a pronunciation aid.

AUTHOR'S NOTE

I offer this play to all who have lost their child, their country, their dreams, their taste for life.

I offer these words to all those forgotten and all who are trying to forget...

to everyone who, every day, every moment, confronts the silence of death.

I would have liked to offer them a glass of water, at least a glass of water..[2]

ABLA FARHOUD

CHARACTERS

MONIQUE/KAOKAB, *between 40 and 50, novelist and playwright, immigrated to North America when she was 9.*

THE MOTHER, *her cousin, also between 40 and 50, a recent immigrant.*

SAMIRA, *the Mother's daughter, around 15 or 16 years old.*

SPACE

A panel representing a map of the world covers the back wall of the stage. A dozen or so drawers are placed at "hot spots" on the map, where wars are today occurring. The drawers, which are accessible from behind the panel, pop open and snap shut throughout the play.

The mappa mundi blends into a large bookcase, the author's library.

Monique/Kaokab's studio occupies most of the stage: a large desk, plants, an ornate chest, and a kitchenette.

The Mother's space, at the extreme upper-right corner of the stage, is described by a single overhead spot. At the opening she is sitting in a rocking chair with her back to the audience. She rocks incessantly, holding a rolled prayer rug which she cradles like a baby. She is wearing a red dress.

Samira darts around the entire theatre, penetrating the protagonists' spaces, scaling the catwalks, or moving through the audience. Her head or hand appear periodically in one or another of the drawers in the backdrop map. She may speak into a microphone which sometimes deforms her voice.

SCENE 1

The entire theatre is dark.

The panting and footsteps of someone running emerge from the darkness at the back of the audience.

Gradually a light comes up on Samira. She is running without moving forward. Arms and legs are attached to her limbs. Shards of flesh stick to her skin. She tries to rip them off. A baby dangles from a rope around her neck.

Music, mixed with the sounds of war, swells.

With all her might, Samira breaks away and runs down the aisle. The baby falls to the ground. She rushes back, picks it up, sticks her fingers in its mouth. The child breathes again. She takes it in her arms and continues to run.

On stage Monique/Kaokab remains riveted to her chair, apparently intent on a game of solitaire set out on her desk. She seems winded, gasping for breath.

Suddenly she jumps up and sweeps the cards to the floor. She paces the room like a caged lion.

MONIQUE/KAOKAB: Solitair...ry confinement. Come on Kaokab, get with it, make your move, I am losing my patience. "In the face of death, any risk is petty."[3] Write, just write, Kaokab.

Samira continues to run. She crosses the stage to the bookcase. She climbs in and out of the drawers.

A spot comes up on the Mother. With her back to the audience, she is sitting in a rocking chair, clutching a rolled prayer rug, cradling it like a baby.

Monique/Kaokab paces back and forth, muttering to herself in search of an inspiration. Her gaze falls on the chest. She approaches, hesitates, and then opens it. She takes out objects and clothing, some photographs that she stares at with emotion. Last she removes a large Oriental rug.

She unrolls the rug. She lies down. She wraps herself in the rug and rolls back and forth as she speaks.

MONIQUE/KAOKAB: (*invoking her family, one by one*) Bayey, Mounir, Samir, Boulos, Kaokab, Amira, Immey.[4]
(*With the father's voice*) *Nemo ya wled, nemo, Allah kbir.*[5]
(*With the mother's voice*) *Allah ma bi sakerha min kil el mayl. Bieyfreyja Allah.*[6]
(*With her natural voice*) We could have been sleeping in the street. We have a roof over our heads. God never closes all doors at once. In winter we could have died of cold. Thank God, it's summer, *noushkor Allah.*[7]
(*With her voice as a child*) Immey, I thought it always snowed here. I love snow because I can roll in it... make snow balls. And I can get warm, warm again when I come home. But I love summer better, because it reminds me of... What's it called Immey? Yeah, Bir Barra, that's it. In Bir Barra we'd eat grapes right off the vine. Are you going to plant some grapes, Bayey? I could pick them like in Bir Barra and eat as many as I want. It would be as good as being there. Same thing.
(*With the father's voice*) It will never be the same, even with a grape arbor. This will never be our country.
(*Child's voice*) It'll be the same, with the grapes, it'll be like our country, huh, Bayey?
(*Mother's voice*) No, Kaokab, never. It will never be our country.

She closes her eyes and falls asleep.

Samira enters. Flesh and limbs are still hanging from her body, but she does not bother to try pulling them off. With the baby in her arms she walks slowly forward, her head high, fearless.
Music and sounds of war grow louder.
A volley of shots. Samira's body stiffens and lifts before falling on Monique/Kaokab sleeping.

The woman wakes screaming. Samira's eyes are riveted on her. Crawling as fast as possible to her desk, Monique/Kaokab writes feverishly.

MOTHER: *Ya waladey... ya waladey... ya waladey...*[8]

Samira has disappeared.

MONIQUE/KAOKAB: (*writing*) She runs. The bodies are piling up...half dead, half alive.... She knows where she's going... she steps over barricades of corpses. The music is calling her, she follows, she moves closer. The baby falls. She picks it up in her arms and breathes life into it again. She wants to die alive, she is no longer running, she has stopped running, she walks toward the music. Drawers slam shut. Drawers fly open. She is walking straight ahead.... She is walking...

Blackout.

SCENE 2

The lights come up on Samira, sitting on a swing high above the stage. Dressed in jeans and a white tee-shirt, she looks like any normal teen-aged girl.

Monique/Kaokab is writing. Frequently she rubs her stomach and her chest. Sometimes she gets up, paces, pours a glass of water, looks up at Samira, before returning to her desk. Her facial expressions often resemble the girl's.

A song by Oum Kalsoum is playing.[9]

SAMIRA: *(swinging)* In my mother's belly I was already getting used to things. That's where I learned how to sing too. (*She begins to hum a lullaby.*)

> *Salam ya Salam, ya, ya albey*
> *Salam ya Salam, ya 'ayouni, ya rouhey*
> *Salam ya Salam, ya waladey...*[10]

I wasn't scared. The explosions don't scare you when your mother is talking and singing softly in your ear. And it's the best way to learn how to count. Even when she was singing, my mother never stopped counting. That's real important. 'Cause if you're not careful, if you forget to count while the bombers are on their business trips right over your head... tough luck. One hit is enough. Without your head you can't count or sing anymore. Maybe it's easier that way.

My mother is still counting. She counts the days, the minutes, the hours, the months, the years, the centuries. I don't need to count anymore. I learned too early and I got sick of it.

Like I got sick of my name. Salam, Salam, Salam...I mean there were too many Salams around. All the mothers seemed to have the same idea the year I was born. Unfortunately Salam is the only name you can give to a boy or a girl. (*Emphatically*) Salam! (*Mimicking a salaam typical of "Hollywood Arabs"*) *Salam alaykoum.* May peace be with you. (*A laugh*) In first grade there were dozens of Salamalaykoums in the class. What a tower of Babel! 'Course we were used to that. Babel, I mean. We lived right in the middle of it.

By second grade we'd all changed our names. No more Salam. It was the only thing we could change, so we did.

To relieve the tension Monique/Kaokab slowly rotates her head, her shoulders, her hips. Her movements resemble a Middle Eastern dance.

SAMIRA: My aunt Kaokab changed her name too. Not for the same reasons. In her school there weren't any Kaokabs at all. Nobody could pronounce her name. They'd say Cow–cab... Corn–cob... Ca...Cacao–bob... and everybody would burst out laughing. In school any silly thing makes you laugh. Somebody farts or a shell explodes and the whole class is rolling in the aisles. In school it doesn't take much to die laughing. So Kaokab decided to change to...Monique. Mo-ni-que. Sounds nothing like Kaokab, does it? Not even the same initials. Me, at least I kept part of my name. Salam Samira, (*with a goofy expression*) Samira salam.

My aunt Monique/Kaokab should have played with her name too. Maybe that's why she hardly ever laughs. No, that's not why. She doesn't laugh because you can't laugh all alone, by yourself. I know something about that. It's easy to cry alone, but just try laughing all by yourself... It looks crazy. How many people have been put away because they laughed alone? But suppose they threw everybody who cries alone in an insane asylum? It would be like millions, I mean just forget it. The asylums could never hold them all. Where I come from there's no more asylum...

Monique/Kaokab pauses in her writing. Samira observes her.

MONIQUE/KAOKAB: No more...a-s-y...a-s-i? A-s-y-l-um... The entire city has become a... an...

SAMIRA: The city has become an...

MONIQUE/KAOKAB:...an open house.

47

SAMIRA: We have become one big open house, a gigantic party, one enormous outdoor asylum, a party big as the country, the continent, and (*radio newscaster's voice*) "the entire Third World." (*Mocking tone*) The Third World. That's what they call us in the West. (*She looks at Monique/Kaokab.*) Does that mean we're one third of the world population or that each of us is one third of a person?

> *Abruptly Monique/Kaokab stops writing. She sorts her papers, picks up the cards scattered on the floor, and rolls up her rug.*

SAMIRA: Uh, oh–h... Looks like this solitaire game is over. Sometimes you need more than patience to play. My aunt's problem is she worries too much. She doesn't laugh enough. She doesn't even cry. So all that stuff stays stuck in her throat. She doesn't know that, from up here, laughing or crying sounds the same. It's just time goes faster when you laugh. Even here. I don't know why that is...
As for my mother, she simply gave up. On life. She cries because it's become a habit, like she used to laugh. 'Course I was the one who made her laugh... My Aunt Kaokab, that's another story. She's so proud. She's always trying to prove she can make it alone. I realized a while back that she really needs my mother.

> *Monique/Kaokab moves toward the Mother. Gently she stops the rocking chair and turns it around to face the audience. Standing behind the chair, Monique/Kaokab puts her arms around the Mother's shoulders and holds her in a long, tender embrace. The Mother seems to expect this and does not react.*

MOTHER: Kaokab, tell me, do you think my daughter would be dead if we had gotten out in time? If my arms had been long enough, if my belly had been big enough, would Samira be alive today?

MONIQUE/KAOKAB: *Ma baaref, ya oum Samira, ma baaref,*[11] I don't know... Come... Come with me.

> *The Mother stands. Monique/Kaokab pushes the rocking chair*

to center stage. The Mother follows, clutching her rolled rug to her chest. Samira, who has left her swing, accompanies them. She hovers behind or twirls in front of the two women. The Mother sits again on the rocking chair. Monique/Kaokab prepares Turkish coffee. Samira flits around her.

MOTHER: Would you please... stop that music.

Monique/Kaokab turns off the music. She brings a tray with a Turkish coffee pot and two small cups, a glass of water, a bowl of sugared almonds. She serves and the two women sip in silence.

MONIQUE/KAOKAB: You'll... you'll be fine here, you'll see.

MOTHER: Sometimes I miss the music of the bombs.

MONIQUE/KAOKAB: My mother used to say, "A man can get used to anything, but never a dog."

MOTHER: No dog lived through what we did. We tied them up. Still, they managed to run away.

MONIQUE/KAOKAB: Animals... animals have a sense of survival... (*She is breathing with great difficulty.*) Humans get lost sometimes, they lose that second sense... They lose... I want to write... a story about that. I've wanted to write about that for a long time.

MOTHER: You write?

MONIQUE/KAOKAB: ...Yes.

MOTHER: You write books?

MONIQUE/KAOKAB: ...Yes.

MOTHER: Many books?

MONIQUE/KAOKAB: (*meaning too many or never enough*) Well, yes...

MOTHER: Why didn't you ever come to see us? That would have made a great book for you.

MONIQUE/KAOKAB: ...You know there are plenty of subjects to write about.

MOTHER: Were you afraid?

MONIQUE/KAOKAB: (*having trouble breathing*) That's... an understatement.

MOTHER: Were you afraid you would be killed?

MONIQUE/KAOKAB:... Worse than that.

MOTHER: What's worse than dying?

MONIQUE/KAOKAB: I just didn't want to die before... before I had... (*in a gasp*) I wanted to choose my death.

MOTHER: Choose your death? What is this planet I have landed on? Choose your death? Did Samira choose her death? Tell me, you, who write therefore you think, did Samira and millions like her choose to die?

MONIQUE/KAOKAB: I... don't know.

MOTHER: You speak madness and then you say I don't know. Your books must be highly entertaining.

> A *pause while they sip their coffee.*

MOTHER: I have been in this country exactly sixty-four days.

MONIQUE/KAOKAB: And me, forty years.

MOTHER: This is the first time I've ever gone out of the house.

MONIQUE/KAOKAB: The first fifteen years my mother didn't

even know the color of the sky here. She never went out to visit, never had coffee with anybody, just to talk. Not even a glass of water... I don't know how she survived.

MOTHER: She became accustomed. You become accustomed to the worst... and then you miss it.

MONIQUE/KAOKAB: (*with a sad smile*) At least you can read and write. And you speak the language.

MOTHER: Knowing a language doesn't mean you can speak... I have said nothing... I don't even know the name of this country.

MONIQUE/KAOKAB: This country can't decide what its name is.[12]

MOTHER: Not to decide, not to have a name is better than to lose it in a blood bath. Samira will never answer to her name, my country lost its name. I have no country, no children.

MONIQUE/KAOKAB: (*trying to calm her*) You're here now, you're safe... far away... You'll be fine here... The problems are less bloody. They get buried in the snow. Here, patience... is still a virtue. You'll be fine here. If you're able to forget.

MOTHER: Never.

They sip in silence.

MOTHER: Why did you come to me?

MONIQUE/KAOKAB: Why? I... don't know... how... to write anymore. This is the first time I...

MOTHER: You write everyday?

MONIQUE/KAOKAB: Just like you feed your family.

MOTHER: Sometimes there was nothing to eat.

MONIQUE/KAOKAB: I haven't been able to write for sixty-four days.

MOTHER: Well, it won't kill you.

MONIQUE/KAOKAB: Are you sure?

MOTHER: Yes, I'm sure.

MONIQUE/KAOKAB: There are many ways to die.

MOTHER: Only one is final.

They sip in silence.

MOTHER: Samira died centuries ago. Four hundred and twenty-nine days ago. At four in the afternoon.

MONIQUE/KAOKAB: It's five to four.

MOTHER: I know. Without looking at the clock, I know... (*With a strange light in her eyes*) I feel her breath... her last breath. I tore my dress to make her a bandage, she was still breathing.

MONIQUE/KAOKAB: (*to herself*) I tore my dress to make her a bandage, she was still breathing... the warmth of her breath. (*Pause.*) Samira was fifteen when she...

MOTHER: She is sixteen years old, two months, and three days... I fought so hard to live... for my children... to live... so we would stay... alive. Alive.

MONIQUE/KAOKAB: (*suffocating*) You do have other children, *noushkor Allah*, you have other...

MOTHER: (*exploding*) Not you too.... Forty years away and you still say "*noushkor Allah*, praise God Almighty," just like those who see the blood pouring from the body next to them, even splashing on them. As long as they are still breathing, they say "thank

God, *noushkor Allah.*" They get used to the worst and the worst does come, because they have already accepted it. *Noushkor Allah, bieyfreyja Allah,* everything is written in the big book, we deserve this, we have so many sins to purge. What sins? To be born there rather than here? Who chooses their birthplace? You, who pretend to choose your death, did you choose your birth? Now there's a subject for one of your books! You know nothing of your mother tongue except these sugar-coated words. I never want to hear them again. Least of all from you.

MONIQUE/KAOKAB: I'm sorry. When... when you don't know what to say, that's what comes to mind... homilies, formulas...

MOTHER: Keep them for your books. An exotic word now and then, that sounds good.

Monique/Kaokab pours another coffee. They drink in silence.

MOTHER: Maybe they are right. I am not alone. Here I have all I need. I have my children. Four healthy children left. But, Kaokab, can a mouth replace an eye? Can a heart do for an ear? Can a nose walk, laugh, dance? My children surround me, they keep me alive, yes, I will not fall to the other side. Yet if all had died, the hole would not be any bigger, the emptiness would not be greater. My soul went with her last breath.

MONIQUE/KAOKAB: You'll be fine here, *ya oum Samira.*

MOTHER: Yes... yes... I don't hear the bombs anymore. Just the snow... the sound of the snow falling... I've always loved snow. I remember a postcard Uncle Walid sent when I was a little girl. I showed it to all my school friends, then I pasted it on the mirror behind the buffet. It was the most beautiful postcard of all. I don't know where it is now. (*With a disturbing light in her eyes*) I don't know where she is now. I don't know... in the flames, the bombs... under the ice, the snow...? Samira... Samira, are you warm, *ya albey*... Are you cold, *ya rouhey*... Are you hungry, *ya 'ayouni*[13]... We have a lot to eat now. Here, water flows from the pipes, hot or cold, you can take as many showers as you want, even a bath.

You can turn on the light, all of the lights if you want. You can play your music all day. You can go to the movies. Samira, you can take classes in movies. We don't have to keep running, to change neighborhoods, cities, countries all the time. We are safe here. You can come and go at whatever hour. You can make movies here, as you wished. The danger has passed, the danger has passed, the danger has passed, there is only snow... snow.

They sip coffee in silence.

MONIQUE/KAOKAB: How are your brothers and sisters?

MOTHER: Scattered. Leaves in the wind. Orphans. Everybody went where they could. My parents stayed behind. They were happy to know we were safe.

MONIQUE/KAOKAB: And the son of your uncle?

MOTHER: You are funny... the way you have kept these old expressions. No one says this "son of your uncle" now. You mean my husband? When Samira left us, so did my husband. He is now only the father of my children. A very good father. He is back there, in a neighboring country. The heat is unbearable. He is like a prisoner, dying a slow death so that his children might survive. He telephones sometimes. Each of the children talks to him, not for too long. Then it's my turn. "How are you?" he asks. I say "Alright and you?" Yes, alright he says. I ask him have you seen Samira, he says yes I have seen Samira. Too much to say or too little, it amounts to the same. He always closes with *"noushkor Allah*, we are alive, that's what counts." I can say nothing. I hear the click. The last time I said praise to God, Samira was still breathing.

Slow fadeout.

SCENE 3

Monique/Kaokab is leaning on the bookcase. She is lost in her thoughts. She breathes with great difficulty.

Samira is somewhere in the audience.

SAMIRA: One day, you don't know why, you just can't take it anymore. You can't, that's all. You can't breathe. I wanted to breathe.

MONIQUE/KAOKAB and SAMIRA: You can't be free and imprisoned, young and old, dead and alive at the same time.

MONIQUE/KAOKAB: At the same time.

SAMIRA: I wasn't asking for the moon, just some peace and quiet. No more orders. I wanted to sleep in my room when I needed to sleep, go out when I felt like it, and visit my friends, Amal and the others, whenever I wanted. That's not a lot to ask, is it? I didn't expect to get a car on my sixteenth birthday, or a camcorder until I got my 16mm. I didn't. I just wanted to take a bath or go see a movie when I felt like it, without waiting for a cease-fire. Those days we didn't know where to start. We were like crazy people released for a day. Or prisoners on the lam. I didn't want anybody telling me what to do and certainly not when to do it. I wanted to be free.
On one raid we ran into a shelter. That was a big change from being outside, right? Most of it was pretty funny. We agreed not to listen to our radios all at once. Everybody was assigned a quarter of an hour. When it was my turn, I tuned in a Bob Dylan song I liked a lot. (*Speaking then singing*) "How many years a man must live before they call him a man?" It was like I was hearing it for the first time. And I saw all of our lives through a zoom lens. "How many stairs a man should climb..."
I felt like throwing up or shitting or dying and I couldn't breathe. At the same time I managed to make everybody laugh. All that at once. My mother held up a sheet to hide me, so I could do all that stuff alone in a big basin that was already full. She was

laughing so much that the curtain slipped and everybody saw my behind... One more naked behind is no big deal... It doesn't change a thing, I know that now.

That time she laughed so much she couldn't help it, but otherwise my mother did everything she could to protect me. I guess that's what mothers are for. She'd put her hands in front of my eyes so I wouldn't see. She couldn't cover my ears at the same time. It became like a game. A weird sort of parlor game. We were all huddled there together, counting the strikes. It was kind of fun. I thought people everywhere lived like that. But when I got older, I began to realize that...un-unh... nay, nay... this couldn't be what life was about. I saw movies which helped me understand, which showed me the difference.

My parents wanted to immigrate, go into exile, I mean just get out! But they couldn't and it's not just because they didn't have enough money. *Bieyfreyja Allah... bieyfreyja Allah...* they kept saying. Wanting to believe. After each raid, they thought that was the last time the sky would dump bombs on our heads. Yeah. My parents grew up in a mountain village, poor things. They still think that day breaks after night, that fruit falls when it is ripe, that the sun shines after the rain, that spring follows winter. Maybe it was like that when they were kids. I saw a lot of my friends go, not die, but leave. Die, I've seen that too, a lot.

We never made it out. Money helps, it sure does. If we could at least have gone on a trip like the rich, until things got better. (*Imitating an affected bourgeoise*) Farewell, my dahlings. I simply cahn't bear it anymore. All that noise has been hell. And all those corpses, it's so depressing. *Au revoir*, dear hearts. You're so quaint. Dead or alive, you don't know the difference do you, poor things? *Ciao mes chéris...* (*She blows kisses right and left.*) My friend Amal didn't have enough money to leave either. Her parents were suckers like mine. Full of hope. So we stayed together longer... I don't know if Amal did it on purpose... I still don't know. You always think some day you'll find the answer...

MONIQUE/KAOKAB: ...You always think some day you'll find the answer. (*She is staring at the Mother.*)

MOTHER: ...You look as if you wanted to eat me alive.

MONIQUE/KAOKAB: (*taking a deep breath*) That little rug.... That look, like someone from another planet, from inner space.... Your eyes...

MOTHER: What are you talking about? What's wrong with my eyes?

MONIQUE/KAOKAB: Ever since I saw you at the airport with your four kids and that little rug you held so tightly.... Ever since... I can't get rid of it.

MOTHER: Why get rid? What do you mean?

MONIQUE/KAOKAB: Nothing... just an expression... I've wanted... (*With a gesture of pulling something from the inside*) For fifteen years I've wanted to write about that.

MOTHER: About my eyes and my rug? That will be a great contribution to literature.

MONIQUE/KAOKAB: I don't know why I keep talking about that, you're not interested anyway.

MOTHER: You're right, I'm not. (*Pause.*) But if you could somehow bring Samira's eyes back, just for an instant, yes, I would be interested, but otherwise...

MONIQUE/KAOKAB: I am not a magician, nor *aafrita* nor *djinia* [14].

MOTHER: *Aafrita, djinia...* You know some rare words. I thought you only remembered "*noushkor Allah.*"

MONIQUE/KAOKAB: I've been reading *Arabian Nights*. There are some words they can't translate.

MOTHER: (*laughing*) If I could still laugh, I would laugh very hard. You learn our language from a translation of *A Thousand and One Nights*. You are so funny... You are a "riot", as my children say. They are learning quickly. Every day they come home with some new expression... While I sit and watch the snow fall, you are reading *Alf laiyla wa laiyla*[15] in a foreign language and my children are absorbing a foreign culture that will become their own culture. It will not be mine or their father's or their grandparents'. They will forget everything...

MONIQUE/KAOKAB: Childhood leaves indelible marks.

MOTHER: Still, they will forget. "Blood does not change to water," they say. No, it doesn't. It dries up and dies. What stayed with you, besides *tabouley*? The memory of the stomach resists, but the rest?

MONIQUE/KAOKAB: (*after a pause*) I remember a song my mother used to sing. And I know a few words: *sharaf, haram, maalesh, boukra, noushkor Allah, leysh, ma baaref, bledna, badi ekol, badi nem, badi mayi, badi mout*[16] ... I remember the smell of the earth, the scent of my mother... I remember her solitude. Nothing else. Nothing.
I learned everything here. I learned winter like you learn arithmetic, with frozen fingers. I learned to blend in, to disappear, to forget. I earn my living in a borrowed language, a language that won't let me cry out. The cries ring false. Even the moans... Pain does not have the same sound. What makes them laugh makes me weep, what makes them weep makes me laugh. I've adapted, I've succeeded as a writer. I write what they like, the royalties from just one of my books would feed three entire villages in Africa or Asia.
I've written the surface of things. To please, to rock people to sleep. I've written to put myself to sleep, to forget. I have written pushing my memory back inside, deep in my stomach. I borrowed a language and I lent my soul. I have lived between the heartbreak of remembering and the heartbreak of forgetting.

MOTHER: I am cold, Kaokab, I'm so cold.

> *Monique/Kaokab gets a blanket and tenderly covers the Mother. The Mother closes her eyes.*
>
> *Slow fadeout.*

SCENE 4

Monique/Kaokab is writing. The Mother is sleeping fitfully. She is muttering inaudible words in her sleep.

Music. Sounds of war.
The music grows louder.

Drawers pop open. Arms, heads, legs are visible. The drawers snap shut.
Other drawers open, revealing eyes, hearts, intestines.
A drawer opens revealing Samira, her head hanging over the edge. It closes and she appears at another drawer.
Blood is streaming over the map.

Monique/Kaokab stops writing. Breathing heavily, she gets up and goes to her rolled rug. She begins kicking it over and over.

MONIQUE/KAOKAB: Why? Why? Why? I'll ask why until the end of time, until my tongue dries up in my mouth. Why her? Why him? Why Beirut? Why them? Why this baby, why Bethlehem? Why that child, why Bir Barra, why our village, our neighborhood, our city, why Babylon, why our country, why our planet? I'll ask why why why until my lungs burst and nobody answers me, nobody will ever answer.
And I want to write! (*Between clenched teeth*) I want to write, God damn it all, I want to stupid fucking write.
(*She takes a few deep breaths, moves to the Mother, and wakes her. The Mother jumps.*) Don't be afraid, it's just me. Mariam... Mariam, do you remember the last meal we ate together?

MOTHER: When you came to visit us? That was over twenty years ago.

MONIQUE/KAOKAB: Where did we go? I can't remember where we were...

MOTHER: It was a restaurant on the beach, in Bir Baroud. There were about twenty of us. There was a slight breeze, a moon, the water at our feet. A hundred little dishes, each one lovelier than the others. Do you remember? You wanted to taste everything. You said: "We are in heaven, eat, eat...before it's all lost. We mustn't waste a bit."

MONIQUE/KAOKAB: (*sadly*) Yes... yes...

MOTHER: And you closed your eyes at each bite. You looked at the sea, you looked at the mountains, and you closed your eyes.... Your eyes were wide open or they were shut tight.

MONIQUE/KAOKAB: It was nineteen years ago.

MOTHER: When the old people in the village saw you, they said, "*Kaokab bint Abou Mounir*[17] left us a young girl and she comes back still a young girl. This must be some American invention, to get younger rather than older. We could use their secrets for our old bones, couldn't we?"

MONIQUE/KAOKAB: I was a little girl when I left. I went back thirteen years later. And now I can't be like the salmon who swim back to die where they were born. The country of my childhood died before me. A wall of fire has cut me off.... (*To herself*) And if I can't write about it... I'll die with it.

MOTHER: "Another eccentric American," they said. "They're all the same, they leave, they come back to visit a few years later. Tourists, foreigners! Didn't they grow up here with the goats and the sheep? Didn't they learn to walk barefoot here on our soil? They act as if they've forgotten everything, our language, even our names. We remember each one of them, but they don't remember a thing." It's true, you'd forgotten everything, your manners, the polite forms. You wore shorts and you muttered phrases nobody could understand. You know very well villagers don't speak any languages but our own. And you would laugh.... Were you making fun of us?

MONIQUE/KAOKAB: Of course not! I'd forgotten my own language. I could have cried, but instead I laughed.... When I was little, I used to cry because I couldn't understand. I learned the word "where" when I was nine years old. I could have laughed... but...

She begins setting the table.

MOTHER: We enjoyed watching you anyway. You would sniff the ground, climb trees, walk around barefoot like a child. Drink water from the village well rather than use our new faucets. And to see you stuff yourself silly with figs and grapes!

MONIQUE/KAOKAB: I knew my childhood was over... I could never go back. It was like making love for the last time. I wanted...

MOTHER: You wanted to see everything, hear everything, do everything. You remember, you made us take you all over. You wore us out playing tourists. And you would shout with pleasure. Our country is beautiful, but shouting like that.... It's over-doing things. (*Pause.*) We could travel anyplace then. We could still move around freely.

MONIQUE/KAOKAB: Really? You had to have an ID card. I remember that struck me... I'd never seen that here.

MOTHER: But we didn't have to show it! Just carry it around. Just a formality. Fear hadn't set in yet. You saw. You were a foreigner, my cousin perhaps, but still a foreigner, and you saw everything we couldn't.

They sit at the table and eat in silence. Samira is perched on the bookcase. Monique/Kaokab looks up at her from time to time and smiles.

SAMIRA: (*as if peering through the eye of a camera*) Seen from this distance human beings are really hilarious. They take them-selves so-o-o serious. Ever since Aunt Kaokab's decided to use me as a character and to look at the world through my eyes, things are going much better. Now, zooming in on human beings... (*She makes a face.*) Sometimes I'd rather just look at ants or bees. Even flies.

Before I thought life was pretty funny too. 'Course, I forced things a little. Just to make life livable. I was always clowning. I liked to do it because people love to laugh. They love you when you make them laugh. Here I don't have to work at that anymore. I see the best bits from the best movies of Charlie Chaplin all the time. On any street, in any house, in any building. In any corner of the world where people are beating each other's brains out over nothing. In every church, every synagogue, every mosque.

Hilarious, I swear, you'd croak laughing. Just take religion for example. Humans always have to find a reason for everything and they always have to be right. Sometimes they fight so long they forget the reason, so they look for another one. But while they're finding the new reason, the other guys are diving head-first into the flames because they still believe in the old reason. Tsk...tsk... you should see them wandering around here in a daze. They don't even remember why they died. Not to know why you're alive is one thing. But not to know why you died... that's really sad.

My friend Amal... I don't even know if she was Catholic, Maronite, Druze, Shiite, Sunnite, Coptic, Greek Orthodox, or Jewish Orthodox. I don't remember and I couldn't care less. What I remember is everything we used to do together and everything we couldn't do. I remember her voice, her eyes that were always full of fear. Her dreams, the poems she wrote, her giggling when I made her laugh so she'd stop crying. I thought she would choke to death, crying and laughing at the same time like that.... But that's not how she died. I know. It's all recorded on film, here, in the eye of my heart.

Monique/Kaokab and the Mother continue to eat in silence. The author is lost in her thoughts. The Mother gazes at the bookcase.

MOTHER: So many books.... To think I spent hours cleaning off the dust.... Four years, three times a week...

MONIQUE/KAOKAB: ...What?

MOTHER: That was my job, cleaning the library. Soon after your visit, I went to work in the city... for a rich family. They always spoke in French.[18] They didn't call me Mariam. It was "Marie! Marie!" all the time. How do you think I learned the language? I had to.

MONIQUE/KAOKAB: So did I.

MOTHER: It's not the same. You left your country. I was in my own country and I had to speak another language to survive. I kept thinking this can't go on. One day the whole thing will...

MONIQUE/KAOKAB: So you too.... You knew it would all blow up.

MOTHER: All I needed was to see their library. Not only were many of the books false, just cardboard, beautiful leather bindings with nothing inside, but all of the real books were in foreign languages. I worked there four years and not once did anyone take a book from the shelf. Not to leaf through it, read it, touch it, not just to say hello to the book. Not once. I would rather read books in my own language, so I searched and searched the shelves. I did not find a single one. Not one. You would have thought we had disappeared without leaving a trace. There was nothing from us, not even a folktale... I get the same feeling looking at your books. Not one is in our language.

MONIQUE/KAOKAB: But I can't read our language.

MOTHER: Why didn't you learn? It didn't seem important? You were seduced like the others, conquered?

MONIQUE/KAOKAB: I was just pushed on a bandwagon that was already rolling. I didn't choose to emigrate. Nobody asked me what I wanted.

MOTHER: Fate never asks what we want. That's the rule. But you keep trying to convince me choice is possible. Who is the one who talked about choosing her own death?

MONIQUE/KAOKAB: Nothing is ever black or white in life.

MOTHER: One thing is irreversible.

MONIQUE/KAOKAB: You're always talking about death. There's not just death. Death is really simple, it's life that...

MOTHER: (*as if stabbed in the stomach*) Death is simple! When you feel it in your flesh, then we'll talk about it. Not before.

MONIQUE/KAOKAB: But I do feel it. Every time someone is killed, torn from life, I die a little. Every time someone is hungry, so am I. Every time someone is humiliated, so am I.

MOTHER: You're lying. That's just a speech by the famous author. When you're hungry, you open your refrigerator and you eat! You only see people die on television. You just get up and turn it on or off. You can still get up. You can move your hand. They can't. For them it's finished. You change channels and you're someplace else and you go on living.

MONIQUE/KAOKAB: You can't expect me to die for real!

MOTHER: That's exactly what I'm saying. It's all in your head.

MONIQUE/KAOKAB: But my head is me. I can't cut it off.

MOTHER: Compassion starts when you get out of your head, when you make a move to help someone.

MONIQUE/KAOKAB: What kind of move? There are so many we could make.

MOTHER: You could have come to see us, but you were afraid of being killed, of dying for real.

MONIQUE/KAOKAB: But you don't understand that grabbing a gun is no solution. It's impossible to take sides.

MOTHER: There were many things to do beside fighting. You preferred to do nothing.

MONIQUE/KAOKAB: Doing nothing is the hardest.

MOTHER: That's not true. The proof is you are still alive and they are dead. No one gave them a glass of water before they died. No one. They are dead and you are still breathing.

MONIQUE/KAOKAB: (*gasping, as if she were struggling not to drown*) *No, no, no!* You're wrong. I can't breathe. It was my country too. It was my childhood too. My feet still run there on the red earth. I have to cut them off and screw them back on my body if I want to live. Don't you get it? I protect myself so I won't die entirely. But the more I protect myself, the farther I move from the bloody mess and the deeper I sink into the imaginary mess, this magma of words. To pick up a gun is so much easier. You don't have to think. You just do it. You kill, you're killed. That's all. But I want to understand. Why this bloody mess? Why such misery? Why. It's been years since I've been able to curl up on my sofa and forget that someplace in the world bodies are burning, people are ripping each other apart, people are starving, people are humiliated, imprisoned, raped, tortured. At the very moment I am trying to find a comfortable position on the sofa, mouths are opening and screaming and I try to plug up my ears because I don't know what to do for them. I want to understand. (*Her tone shifts.*) Yes, I'm scared. Yes, I'm afraid of dying. I don't want to die for nothing. I don't want to die before I've written. I don't want to die before I've understood.

MOTHER: There's nothing to understand. It's human destiny.

MONIQUE/KAOKAB: *No, no, no.* Destiny is an easy word. I want happiness to be possible. I want to change our destiny. Christ, will I ever finish this fucking play? Will it ever be over?

MOTHER: What are you talking about?

MONIQUE/KAOKAB: About this goddamned life that no one can live anymore. Never a moment of peace, a time to rest, that's over for everybody, whether their country is at peace or in the middle of a war. And I'm not just talking about myself! Our thoughts are constantly short-circuited. Our planet, a thousand times more complex than my computer, where every little flea, every ant, every human being, every tree has its place, we're all stuck in this together... I want happiness to be possible.

MOTHER: Happiness!

MONIQUE/KAOKAB: (*with unleashed fury*) Yes, happiness, yes, the simple pleasure of living, of just feeling alive, like a stupid cat arching its back as long as it can still move.... We know too much and not enough.... Closing your eyes hurts as much as opening them. My neighbor may live on the other side of the earth, he's still my neighbor. My eyes are open and I don't know what to do.... There's too much to do.... Every country at war is my country... I want happiness to be possible... I don't want the awareness of others to stop us from having a life. Happiness is nothing to be ashamed of. You have to breathe in life, like the tree sucks water from the ground.

MOTHER: (*cynical*) So that's why you never came to see us.... You were afraid of losing your little piece of happiness?

MONIQUE/KAOKAB: (*furious*) You are really a pain in the ass. You don't understand anything. You talk about compassion and you can't even put yourself in my place, not for one second. Understanding means reaching out to someone, hugging them close, even in your mind. You don't have room for that, you're so full of your own suffering and you won't give up an inch. You're proud of it. It makes you tall, superior. It gives you every right. You talk from the lofty heights of your grief as if you were the only one who had ever lost anything. Draped in your flaming red robes, you suffer. You didn't want to wear black, because you refuse to face the facts. It's time to mourn, Mariam, that means leaving a little opening for life to return, stop blaming everybody for your pain, that means accepting life, even with the missing pieces.

MOTHER: Never, you hear, never.

MONIQUE/KAOKAB: You have to. So do I.

MOTHER: Do as you please. I can never accept this.

MONIQUE/KAOKAB: Mariam, life isn't a contest with a prize for the one who suffers the most. If that's what you think, rest assured, many suffer, too many, and they don't all have the satisfaction of locating the wound. They are bleeding inside.

MOTHER: So am I.

MONIQUE/KAOKAB: You know where it comes from, you know why, you're luckier than us. All those you see out there, walking calmly through the falling snow, they don't know why they suffer, but they do.

MOTHER: Nobody here knows what it means to see your country on fire, nobody knows what it means to see your child buried alive...

MONIQUE/KAOKAB: ...You think they're stupid assholes? They know. They're just trying to forget. Life is hard enough as it is. You should understand, in our language "insen" means human and forget, the same word. If we couldn't forget, just a little, we'd die or go crazy, if we let ourselves feel to the fullest, we'd die or go crazy... we forget, we have to forget... but we don't know it's useless. We're still eaten from the inside, we still can't live our life, we still ache with solitude. Sure, we forget, but it's of no use.... Whatever we do, an invisible thread is spinning between you, Samira, and all of us.... (*Her eyes closed as if praying*) I want to reveal this invisible thread. I have to write the invisible.

SCENE 5

Samira is walking on a tight rope above the audience.

SAMIRA: Everything was okay when Amal was alive. It was still okay then. We could see each other when school wasn't closed, and we could talk as long as the telephones weren't cut off. It wasn't so bad. You can get used to anything, or almost. I wanted to make a movie about that. I had my topic... two friends who accomplish an impossible feat, who, working together against all odds keep their good humor. I didn't want to do a big Hollywood production, just a simple film about how two ordinary girls manage to overcome anything, absolutely-lutely anything, just because they love each other. I didn't need to invent a lot, just condense our lives, shorten our conversations. We'd see the streets of the city with lots of kids playing, the houses, the lovely old homes that were left, and the ugly new ones they kept building to replace them. Some wounded people maybe, but no corpses... they rot too fast and smell even faster. We'd have some beautiful close ups of Amal, with her long black hair shining in the sun. A neat little film, low budget, easy to shoot. Amal would have the star role. Maybe I'd have a stand-in for me. It's hard to be behind the camera and in the picture. Woody Allen does that, but he has a lot of experience. This would be my first film.

My mother was happy I was going to be a director. She doesn't like to read but she loves to watch movies. My father thought it was a man's profession. Like war? I asked him. He dropped the subject. What I like about my father is he doesn't try to prove he's right when he knows he's not. He's really cool. He just said, "*Inshallah* [19]... we'll see." He was hoping someday the (*spelling the word out*) W–A–R would leave us in peace. Dream on. One of them lasted a hundred years. Just one silly war. I learned that in school. I learned about the Vietnam war in the movies. The Americans came back in pieces and then made movies about it. Others did, not the ones in pieces.

You can't make movies when you're in pieces. Just look at my mother.... She won't make a movie about the war. But my aunt will. Yet... I don't know if movies or plays or books can change anything... I don't know... I haven't been here long enough.... Did one ever make a tank turn back? Or stop a bomber from unloading its crap? Has a single bomb ever changed its mind because of a film, a play, or a book? No?... I didn't think so. It helps the guys who write and direct and act, yeah, it helps them let off steam.

People in Europe and America have made movies about us, but we never saw any of them. They say it's to "alert public opinion." (*A laugh*) Alert public opinion.... From up here that's the biggest joke of all.

Blackout.

*The notes of an Arab flute [*nay*] solo are heard in the dark.*

SCENE 6

*Night. Monique/Kaokab paces the floor and then returns to her
desk where a game of solitaire is laid out. The Mother joins her.*

MOTHER: You can't sleep?

MONIQUE/KAOKAB: I can't write. So I'm playing solitaire. It helps
pass the time. Watch time passing. Stop time. It inspires me.

MOTHER: One of those queer writer's habits?

MONIQUE/KAOKAB: If you want to call it that.... Every time I
lay out the cards, the possibility of a new life opens. The worst
thing is stagnation. You have to keep the movement going, any
movement, even if it makes no sense. In solitaire you have
what is hidden and what is given, what you have to grasp immediately and what takes more patience. I've been playing at least
thirty years and I have never seen the same combination appear
twice, never the same life. The end is always the same, of course.
The most enviable life or the most wretched, they all wind up
in the flocks of the dead. That's the rule. So I shuffle the cards
again. Some day I'll write a story about each set. A book for each
life. They're all worth it.

MOTHER: Spread out the cards. Show me Samira's life.

MONIQUE/KAOKAB: Samira is dead. You can't go on living as
if she were alive.

MOTHER: Don't worry about that. It's my problem. I just want
you to tell me the story. Isn't that your job? You bring things to
life, places and people to life, so go ahead. Tell me the story of
Samira's life.

MONIQUE/KAOKAB: I never learned how to tell stories. I just
learned how to write... in a foreign language, remember?

MOTHER: Just between us. I'm not going to record your words....

Just to pass the night away.

MONIQUE/KAOKAB: Story telling and writing are two very different things.

MOTHER: If you wish, I will open the game. I will tell your story.

MONIQUE/KAOKAB: (*in a bad mood*) I already know my story.

MOTHER: But I don't. So I will tell it and that way I can learn it.

MONIQUE/KAOKAB: I'd rather play solitaire.

MOTHER: Play while I tell the story. Once upon a time, in a country far away, a country with no borders and no name, a little girl...

MONIQUE/KAOKAB: (*She cuts her off with a surly voice.*) You're wrong. My country had a name.

MOTHER: Go on with your solitaire if you like, but don't interrupt me. In a country with no name and no borders, a little girl was born. She had no name. She was the eighth girl of the family. The eighth daughter! All her sisters had been given the names of their grandmothers and great-grandmothers. There was one great-grandmother whose name had not been taken, but no one could remember it because she had died very young, may God forgive her. So all the inhabitants of this country, although they had many other things to do just to stay alive, God willing, braving the locusts which, without pity, ravaged the crops, confronting the invaders who, with even less pity, ate everything the locusts, by the goodness of their souls, had forgotten... So all the inhabitants of this country, from the smallest to the biggest, searched, from morning to night, searched without resting to find the name of the forgotten great-grandmother. And the little girl who had no name, may God help her, waited and waited. Then one day, when she...

MONIQUE/KAOKAB: I'm going to bed.

MOTHER: You're giving up. You're afraid to tell Samira's story, aren't you?

MONIQUE/KAOKAB: But she's dead!

MOTHER: That's exactly why you should tell her story.

MONIQUE/KAOKAB: It won't bring her back to life.

MOTHER: (*in pain and anger*) No, it won't bring her back, but I need to hear her name spoken by someone beside me. I don't want to be the only one who remembers she existed, that she was alive, so alive, so beautiful it made you breathless, so funny she could make a foreigner forget his own country. Sparkling like the morning dew. Her voice cut through the darkness of our lives. She was alive and they killed her, they killed my child...

MONIQUE/KAOKAB: (*taking her in her arms*) Stop torturing yourself. Stop. You can't ask the world to suffer in your place, nobody can remember in your place. You are your own memory and you will die with it.

MOTHER: (*crying out*) No. I don't want her death to be lost. I want her death to serve life. I want her body mixed with my tears to nourish our memory. I want her blood to give birth. I want... I want... I want...

MONIQUE/KAOKAB: So do I, *ya oum Samira*, but what can...

MOTHER: (*with great force*) Kaokab, if you don't want to tell her story, then write it. Write, I don't care in what language, just write.

MONIQUE/KAOKAB: (*helplessly*) I've tried... I have... I can't do it. Everything I write is trivial compared to the knot in my stomach, compared to the lava drowning the world. I know that memory can only be carried down through art, literature, true art, but I just can't find the way.

MOTHER: You have to. That's all. You have to.

MONIQUE/KAOKAB: I can't... I can't...

The Mother runs to the desk. She ruffles through the papers feverishly.

MOTHER: All these words? In all these words there must be one shaped like a knife, one that is stronger than the silence of death.

Monique/Kaokab picks up the pages, looks at them, looks into the distance, and then reads.

MONIQUE/KAOKAB: (*reading*)

I learned of war through a distorting lens
from images dreams nightmares and guilt
I learned of war through each of my own who displaced disoriented
exiled
one after another
and those who could not escape
and those who lived with blind hope

I learned of war by turning away
I learned of war by refusing to see or to hear
I learned of war by covering my ears
and pretending to go on living
I learned of war through denial and tearing up the newspaper
I learned of war in spite of my constant refusal to learn
I learned of war on my childhood
on my peaceful red village
shattered to pieces occupied territory

I learned that innocence was dead forever
that eviscerated bodies can be used for barricades
piled one on the other in a reeking mountain

Sitting at my desk
I wonder what they did with all the smelly corpses
I wonder sitting at my desk can you be numbed to the stench of
the corpses

*does a heart smell like a foot, an eye, or a gut
do the flies, the roaches, the rats prefer fresh meat
do the flies roaches rats wait until the soul breaks free and
rises
can the soul find its way through the smoke of the street
or does the soul suffocate too*

*Sitting at my desk clutching to my indispensable
objects, I wonder do dogs and cats still live in the streets
of Beirut Babylon Bethlehem
do dogs and cats like to lick human blood
have the dogs and the cats become used to the sound of bombs
of machine guns of children crying of the wounded screaming
of a woman wailing the loss of her first born
does the wailing change when it's the third or the fourth
child who gives up the last drop of blood to the pavement
does the father, the mother, the grandmother have any tears left
where is the hidden fountain
does a day come when the body hands in its resignation saying
"sorry I don't want to fight anymore"*

*Is life stronger than death
do flowers still grow in tin cans along the balconies
of Bethlehem Baghdad Beirut
are there any window panes left
are there still children playing in the streets
do they wait until the corpses are removed or do they use them as
toys, playing at war or building empires,
constructing fortresses of human flesh*

*Are their blocks their dolls their balls and their trucks
forever stained with blood
in the streets of hundreds of towns zillions of
flies have sucked the blood of millions of boys killed by their
brothers while their sister sat at her desk, writing or not,
weeping in silence*

*In the streets of hundreds of towns scorching the world
rats and flies and roaches and bugs of all kinds*

are licking their chops preparing to feast

*In the aseptic offices of a few dozen cities they're licking
their chops, rats of all kinds,
counting their yen their marks their dollars and pounds*

*In the streets of hundreds of Babylons throughout the world
flies rats and roaches suck on the toes of children who cannot
swat them away and meanwhile I write or I don't,
I weep and say nothing*

*In the houses of hundreds of cities children open their toy
chests and scratch their head choosing a game that will distract
them for a few minutes and meanwhile I write or I don't
I weep and say nothing
and in those cities bright colored garbage cans
the pantry of a million anonymous people
without name, or address, or country,
they are silent as I am today,
I have stopped writing, I have stopped crying, I
say nothing.*

*A long pause. Monique/Kaokab returns to her game of soli-
taire. The Mother stands staring at her. She seems naked without her rug in her arms.*

MOTHER: Where's Samira in all that? I didn't see her.

MONIQUE/KAOKAB: She was in every single word.

MOTHER: But I want to hear her name. I want you to talk about
her, not your silly writer problems.

MONIQUE/KAOKAB: Do you really want me to tell Samira's story?

MOTHER: Yes, I do.

MONIQUE/KAOKAB: The real Samira? Your child? My child?

The child of the whole planet?

MOTHER: Yes, that's what I want.

MONIQUE/KAOKAB: (*firmly, enunciating each syllable*) *Ya oum Samira*, your daughter Samira, our child, held her head high, kept her eyes wide open and marched straight through the mine field. She chose her own death. (*The Mother's head reels under the shock.*) Samira chose her own death.

MOTHER: *Khawta bil marra* [20]! *Khawta bil marra*! You are crazy! You are completely mad!

> The Mother picks up her rug and heads for the door. Monique/Kaokab holds her back. She tries to wrench the Mother's rug away. They struggle.

MONIQUE/KAOKAB: Samira didn't want to die piece by piece, eaten away by fate. She wanted a real death. She wanted to make a choice, just once in her life, to decide her god damned destiny.

SAMIRA: Yes, I said no. No more hope. Hope had become a bad habit.
Like a drug that's lost its effect.
I said no when my friend Amal died. 'Course I'd seen dozens die. But Amal's hit me head on, crushed my lungs, slashed my heart open, cut off my feet, ripped out my tongue.
Amal decided for me. Did *she* have a choice?
I lived in the muck. To go on living was to give up. I decided to die. I broke the contract I had with life. Life never kept its part of the bargain, I don't see why I should have.

MONIQUE/KAOKAB: When Amal died Samira knew she could-n't go on.... To go on living would have been to give up...

MOTHER: Who is Amal?

MONIQUE/KAOKAB: (*without missing a beat*) Her friend who was killed, tortured, raped, torn to pieces. The one they had to tie together to bury. Samira saw her with her eyes open.... She saw Amal...

MOTHER: Samira had many friends, many friends who died. None of them were named Amal.

MONIQUE/KAOKAB: Her name isn't important. Her name was Amal, Amira, Anne, Suzanne, Salam, Sylvia, whatever.

MOTHER: No, there's no "whatever." If you don't know anything, then keep your mouth shut.

MONIQUE/KAOKAB: But you wanted me to...

MOTHER: (*furious*) To speak is not to lie. To write is to tell the truth.

> *Monique/Kaokab grabs her papers and searches as if she were looking for the truth. She begins to read. Her voice changes little by little. She begins to resemble Samira.*

MONIQUE/KAOKAB: That morning I left for school, like any non-normal day when there was a cease-fire. My mother had made *aarouss*, she always said "aarouss" like in the village, not sandwich like everybody else in town. Bread and black olives with a little olive oil, the same kind we ate everyday. We complained sometimes, just as a game. "Oh, no not olives again!" "If your grandparents didn't have the olive trees, I don't know where we'd be today. *Noushkor Allah*, we still have olives, *noushkor Allah*. And they're good for your health."
But nobody said anything that day. I hadn't said anything for a long time. I waited for the bus with my brothers and sisters, as usual. Mother watched from the balcony, as usual. We lived on the fourth floor. I looked up... for the last time... I'd been walking around with my eyes shut for months... I saw my mother bend down and run her hands through the perfume plant she'd brought from her village... she caressed the leaves and brought her hands to her nose. She stayed that way for a long time with her eyes closed, breathing the perfume. All of a sudden she opened her eyes like a bee stung her, she saw us, she turned

toward me, she looked at me...

MONIQUE/KAOKAB and SAMIRA: She looked at me... (*rapidly*) and then we climbed on the bus.

SAMIRA: There was a cease-fire that day... the 942nd one... Nobody thought it would hold, but everybody pretended it would... you had to lie to yourself to... I don't know whose plan it was that day, whether it was an American plan or Russian, Zionist, Baasist, Falangist or whatever... a cease-fire of the allies or the enemies.... We didn't even know the difference between allies and enemies anymore. We didn't know who was calling the shots. The devil himself seemed to be holding the camera. Wide-angle shots, 360° panoramas at break-neck speed... only the devil could move that fast. Human beings, with or without Satan, have always been more gifted for war plans than for peace plans. I mean even in the movies, look at all the special effects and stuff used for the big blasters.... For a movie about life... all you need is a little camera, a few spots to light the actors' faces. (*Pause.*) I decided to do my own film, to call my own shots, to see with my own eyes... or close the lens when I wished. I wanted to see from above, below, all sides, close up, zoom in, zoom out, distant shot and fade out...

MOTHER: No. It's not true. Samira loved life too much to...

MONIQUE/KAOKAB: Maybe that's why she did it. She loved life too much. So she took the plunge...

MOTHER: No no no no no no no. They killed her. They killed her. They tore the life from her body.

MONIQUE/KAOKAB: You're right, they killed her. If Samira had lived someplace else, she wouldn't have marched toward the music of the bombs, that music she knew so well. She wouldn't have run from street to street looking for the death machine. No, Samira, like so many others who love life too much, who will not settle for anything less, would have gone home, locked the bathroom door, filled the bath tub with hot water, taken a shiny little object that makes no noise, and sunk into the scalding water....

She sank into the heat... peacefully... *ya oum Samira*, your child, my child, our earth child was swept away in the steaming lava.

MOTHER: You really want to finish me for good.

MONIQUE/KAOKAB: No, I just want to understand.... What holds us to life... with all its misery? Why a certain day do we decide that's enough? Why do we draw the line that day? Why do we cut the thread that instant? We could have done it a thousand times before... why do we say, at that instant, we cannot, we will not go on?

> *Disarmed, ravaged, the Mother walks around the room. Monique/Kaokab picks up her rug and unfolds it slowly. She sets a brass tray filled with apples on the rug. She gestures, inviting the Mother, and sits on the rug. After a long pause the Mother joins her. The two women look at each other a long moment. Monique/Kaokab holds out her arms. The Mother offers her prayer rug. Monique/Kaokab cradles the rug and sings.*
>
> *During the following scene and accelerating until the end of the play, bodies fall from the drawers, the bookcase, the flies. They fall around and sometimes touch the two women who become increasingly serene. The bodies fall into a mountain of inert flesh. Then rise, scale the walls, and fall again. The* Abou Zoulof *melody Monique/Kaokab initiates shifts and swells until the end of the play.*

MONIQUE/KAOKAB: (*singing*)

> *Haiyhat ya bou zoulof*
> *Aayni ya moulaya*
> *Ya alb safeyr ma 'aou*
> *Ta trajey'ao leya*
> *La tahzaney 'al heyjr*
> *Ya 'ayney la 'dhoubey*
> *Mahma yagheyb el badr*
> *Wa 'ateymo el droubey*[21]

MOTHER: (*smiling sadly*) So you haven't forgotten everything...

Monique/Kaokab smiles. A pause. She asks permission to open the prayer rug. The Mother nods. Monique/Kaokab unfolds the rug, admires it, strokes it tenderly.

MONIQUE/KAOKAB: It's beautiful.

MOTHER: Samira always kept it with her.

MONIQUE/KAOKAB: It's very beautiful.

MOTHER: Yours too, it's beautiful.

MONIQUE/KAOKAB: It's the one my mother brought with her when she came. It was a wedding present from her parents. We slept on it over a year. Then we got beds. (*Pause.*) Would you like an apple?

MOTHER: I'd like some grapes from our fields. I'd like to eat them with my hands full of dirt, sitting on the ground, watching the horizon slip far, far away, beyond the third mountain. I want to be a child again. I want to erase everything and start all over.

MONIQUE/KAOKAB: Look at this apple. Isn't it lovely? It grew here. Try it at least.

MOTHER: How can anything grow under all this snow?

MONIQUE/KAOKAB: Snow melts. Winter always comes to an end.

MOTHER: You believe that?

MONIQUE/KAOKAB: Everything comes to an end.

MOTHER: Samira's life, did it come to an end?

MONIQUE/KAOKAB: Samira's life was stolen from her. That's not the same thing. It's an abnormal cycle... which has lasted a few aeons.

MOTHER: Kaokab, tell me, do you think it will end one day? Is there any more room in our bones and our hearts for suffering? Does pain also die and make room for something else?

MONIQUE/KAOKAB: Everything has an end, I think so, *ya oum Samira.* If a book is written, then begin another. You can't erase the first one, start from zero, be little again. You have to go on. Keep growing. Keep learning. Stick your foot in the crack which will somehow open things up. We are all very vain... me especially. To think that I can carry down my memory or that of my own is the height of vanity... but I have to try... I don't want to be crushed.... Pain is everywhere, but so is life, it's irrepressible, here, there, everywhere... despite the odds... I don't want to drown... go under, maybe, but come up again... I want to write as long as I am alive.

> *She holds out the tray again. The Mother takes an apple, rolls it in her hands, brings it to her nose, and breathes deeply with her eyes closed.*

> *The bodies continue falling, rising, scaling the wall. Samira's voice rises over the music.*

SAMIRA: In my mother's belly I learned to count, to sing, to get used to things. In the belly of the earth I am learning how to laugh. All by myself. I am learning the game of patience. *El sabr meyfteh el faraj.*[22] Is patience the secret to finding the light?

> *The lights come down.*

> *The music continues.*

$\sim$

NOTES

1. From the 1989 *Webster's Encyclopedic Unabridged Dictionary of the English Language*, New York: Gramercy Books.

2. Read by the author at the premiere of *Jeux de patience*, Théâtre de la Licorne, Montreal.

3. From a Spanish proverb.

4. Monique/Kaokab invokes her family, beginning with *bayey* [papa], listing the proper names of her brothers and sisters, and ending with *immey* [mama].

5. *Nemo ya wled, nemo, Allah kbir.* [Sleep, children, sleep. God is great.]

6. *Allah ma bi sakerha min kil el mayl. Bieyfreyja Allah.* [God never closes all doors at once. God will deliver you.]

7. *Noushkor Allah.* [Thank God. Praise be to God.]

8. *Ya waladey* [Oh, my child.]

9. The famous Egyptian singer Oum Kalsoum (or Koulsom) was a living legend in the Middle East. Her recordings have remained popular throughout the Arab world.

10. *Salam ya albey/ ya 'ayouni/ ya rouhey/ ya waladey...* [Peace my soul, my eyes, my heart, my child....] Throughout her monologue Samira plays with the multiple meanings of *salam* as her given name, as peace and its ironic opposite, as a common greeting or an Orientalist projection of the Arab.

11. *Ma baaref, ya oum Samira, ma baaref.* [I don't know, oh mother of Samira, I don't know.]

12. The country which has not chosen its name is a reference to Quebec's ambiguous status, or that of any minority nation within a nation-state.

13. *Ya albey... ya rouhey...ya 'ayouni* [My heart, my soul, my eyes.]

14. *Aafrita* [she-devil], *djinia* [genie]. Monique/Kaokab pronounces the words in a hesitant rendition of classic Arabic. The Mother pronounces the words in popular spoken Arabic.

15. *Alf laiyla wa laiyla* translates literally as "A Thousand and One Nights".

16. The list of words Monique/Kaokab remembers is: *sharaf, haram, maalesh, boukra, noushkor Allah, leysh, ma baaref, bledna, badi ekol, badi nem, badi mayi, badi mout* [honor, forbidden, no matter, thank God, tomorrow, why, I don't know, our country, I want to eat, I want to sleep, I want some water, I want to die].

17. *Kaokab bint Abou Mounir.* [Kaokab, daughter of the father of Mounir.]

18. The use of French or English by the local bourgeoisie is a common fact throughout the postcolonial world.

19. *Inshallah.* [God willing. God knows.]

20. *Khawta bil marra!* [You are crazy!]

21. *Haiyhat ya bou zoulof/ Aayni ya moulaya/ Ya alb safeyr ma 'aou/ Ta trajey'ao leya/ La tahzaney 'al heyjr/ Ya 'ayney la 'dhoubey/ Mahma yagheyb el badr/ Wa 'ateymo el droubey.*
Abou zoulof is a Lebanese folk song with a plaintive melody. The first two lines are opening calls which cannot be translated. Loosely translated the following lines are: "My heart goes with him/ To bring him back again to me/ Don't be sad because of this exile/ My eye does not melt away/ In spite of the waning moon/ And the darkening path."

22. An Arabic saying: *El sabr meyfteh el faraj* means "Patience is the key to deliverance," which the author interprets as "Patience is the key to the light."

PRONUNCIATION AID

The following key should be used as an initial aid to pronunciation and not a substitute for oral coaching. The transliteration is based on the French script and the author's pronunciation of popular Lebanese Arabic. Any Arabic dialect may be used since the play is not geographically specific.

Kaokab: roughly *cow-cob*

ey (bayey, waladey): the French é or as in "pay"

i (bi): as in "to be"

min rhymes with "pin"; *bint* rhymes with "mint"

ou (noushkor, boukra): as in "soup" or "pool"

aa (baaref) or *'a (ya 'ayouni)*: Arabic *'ain* sound

aiy (laiyla): as in "eye"

kh (khwata): as in German "ach"

WEREWERE LIKING

THE
WIDOW DYLEMMA

Translated from the French by

JUDITH G. MILLER

UBU REPERTORY THEATER PUBLICATIONS
NEW YORK

Werewere Liking, painter, poet, novelist, composer, director and playwright, was born in Cameroon in 1950 and has been living in Ivory Coast since 1980. Thanks to her grandmother, she received a grounding in the oral and ritual traditions of the Bassa culture, a knowledge which inspired her to create a new theatrical aesthetic based on African rituals. After staging a number of original dramatic works with her students at the University of Abidjan, she founded the Ki-Yi group in 1983 with her French colleague, Marie-José Hourantier, and three actor-composer-choreographers. Since 1985, when Hourantier left to create her own theatrical group, the Ki-Yi has developed into a unique community where some fifty artists, from eight different African countries, perform on a daily basis and run an art gallery, a museum, a publishing house, a restaurant and boutiques, as well as a theater. Werewere Liking, whose plays include *Une nouvelle terre, Du sommeil d'injuste* (1980), *Singue Mura* (1991) and *Un Touareg s'est marié à une Pygmée* (1992), also designs the sculptures, jewelry and costumes for the group's productions. As Ki-Yi's Artistic Director, her purpose is to create a Pan-African aesthetic using giant puppets, masks, shadow shows, the physical and mental training derived from initiation rituals, traditional memorization techniques, African music and chants. Werewere Liking's writings and the work of the Ki-Yi are known internationally thanks to the group's tours in Europe (annually at the Limoges Festival in France), Japan, North America and Africa. Werewere Liking was awarded the Arletty Prize for her contribution to French-language theater in 1991 and the 1993 Fonlon-Nichols Prize for her contribution to the arts.

La Veuve Diyilem (*The Widow Dylemma*) was originally written for Ki-Yi Village actress Marie-Philomène Nga.

Judith G. Miller, Director of the Paris Center of Critical Studies (1992-1994), is also on the faculty of the Department of French and Italian at the University of Wisconsin-Madison. She is the author of numerous articles on contemporary French and Francophone theatre, a book on theatre and politics (*Theatre and Revolution in France Since 1968*, French Forum, 1977), on Françoise Sagan (Twayne, 1988) and, with Christiane Makward, a forthcoming anthology of translated plays *Plays by French and Francophone Women: A Critical Anthology* (The University of Michigan Press, 1994). Her translations of Ina Césaire's *Island Memories* (with Christiane Makward) and *Fire's Daughters* have been produced at Ubu Repertory Theater. The latter appears in a recent Ubu publication: *New French-Language Plays* (1993).

The Widow Dylemma, in Judith G. Miller's translation, had its first staged reading at Ubu Repertory Theater, 15 West 28th Street, New York, NY 10001, on April 25th, 1994.

CHARACTERS

LONDE, *the widow Dylemma* [1]

HER HUSBAND, *off-stage voice*

THE DIRECTOR, *stage directions which take the form of a silent but persuasive dialogue with the characters*

A TV ANCHORWOMAN, VARIOUS GOVERNMENT MINISTERS, TELEVISION PERSONALITIES, EXTRAS [2]

---

[1] "Londè" in the Bassa language means "wedding band," "union," "intimacy." "Dylemma," [Diyilem] also Bassa, means "that which is predictable," "that whose functioning we understand." The proper names were chosen for their ironic impact, "Dylemma," more particularly because of the wordplay it permits. (T.N.)

[2] In the original production, these characters appeared in video clips. Londè turned on and off the television by remote control. (T.N.)

The story takes place in the prison-like atmosphere of a bourgeois living room. Two large armchairs, a television, a mirrored door, and a framed standing photograph of the deceased husband are prominent in the stage action.

DIRECTOR: *After nine months away, you're finally back home Londè! You've just closed your door as if afraid of an unwelcome visitor, an impromptu interruption! You throw your suitcase in the corner. And now, at last, you're free, alone! What will you do? You study your prison-like, "nouveau riche" living room. You're astonished at having forgotten certain details that meant so much such a short time ago: the large television screen in the middle of the room with the photo of your husband perched on top—your husband, whose death imposed nine months of traditional mourning from which you have just emerged! You walk towards the photograph, look at it a moment and place it face down while murmuring:*

LONDE: Not now, not yet, please!

DIRECTOR: *The mirror on your husband's bedroom door, which reflects the entire living room, shows you in your mourning dress of indigo blue; yet the ceremony which concluded the mourning period took place three days ago! How could you still be dressed in these clothes you hate so much? What magical symbolism ties and holds you to them? Near your armchairs, also covered in batik (indigo blue with white radiating circles), a mysterious harmony envelops you. Moved, you turn away from the mirror. Yes, you'd forgotten the details!!! The sunbeams which light each piece of furniture individually as if to bestow each one with a life of its own, but also the thin covering of dust, like a mist, a trace of powder which always layered everything during your vacations. With your finger, you write on a piece of furniture: "dilemma!" Then you stand up, your arms hanging at your sides. What will you do now? Dust? Sweep? You walk towards a door, hesitate, change directions, go towards another one, and then on to another. You return compulsively to your husband's bedroom door...*

LONDE: I'd forgotten the impression that door made on me,

no—it's the mirror! It always managed to turn people away. It must have been put there to draw attention elsewhere. Facing it, you saw the space behind you, or looked at yourself, and you forgot to move forward; you didn't dare knock. How do you knock on a mirror, anyway? A door isn't a mirror.... A mirror is a door to yourself, not to another person!

DIRECTOR: *You remember now all the times when you stopped there, disarmed. There are just too many things you've forgotten in only nine months away: wasn't it more like nine years? Luckily, it's not total amnesia: you didn't forget your plump balloon armchairs, on which in happy moments the two of you used to jump, face to face, like children on a trampoline. You stared at each other until, like magnets, you were irresistibly drawn together. And during those nine trying months, you projected yourself back here over and over again to your armchair in order to feel propelled by the springs of the powerful desire that filled you then, and rebounded again and again until you were dizzy, until all your senses were alive! And now you turn and twirl, carried away. Which moments took you to that chair? How many times were you launched towards a lost paradise?*
How long have you been unconscious? A minute? An eternity? Here you are, slumped, spiritless, halting. A hard object under the seat bothers you: it's the remote control of your large-screen television! Just a minute! You'd also forgotten how many times you'd felt you'd failed and had automatically turned on the TV! As if you had no other choice, you repeat the same gesture... These words, "the Honorable Minister of Economics of the Chamber for International Exchange (MECIE)," appear over an image of a woman dressed in yards and yards of cloth, each layer threatening to drown her with every rattling breath she painfully takes. You missed her first words and you turn up the volume.

THE HONORABLE MECIE: As a result, if Damas hadn't invaded the Gaffe, the Untied Estates wouldn't have had such a great opportunity to launch the Coalition of Fifty-Two Brutes, and the stock market wouldn't have had such a spectacular shot in the arm...

TV ANCHORWOMAN:...You just heard the concluding remarks of the Minister of Economics of the Chamber for International

Exchange—or "MECIE," as ordinary folks like to call our iron lady who doesn't mince words. And if we've understood her correctly, we should also say, "Thank you Damas. One man's misfortune is lots more fortune for somebody else." *(She turns the page.)* The activities of the U.N.'s International Women's Week dominate the rest of the news: "We should indeed spoil all our mothers and sisters this week," declared the Minister of Man's Fate in Feminine Form (MOFF). He set the tone immediately in his reassuring address. Let's listen to him.

THE HONORABLE MOFF: Mothers and sisters, I hear you! Peace means only one thing: keep it up!

TV ANCHORWOMAN: Keep it up, yes indeed! Dear sisters, now we present a selection of key statements from our government officials most concerned with women's issues. First we'll hear from the Head of the Department of Women's Trade at the Ministry of Industry, then from the Minister of Territorial Administration, and finally from the Minister of the Interior...

HEAD OF THE DEPARTMENT OF WOMEN'S TRADE: My dear sisters, everything considered, I'm for liberated women—completely liberated, perfectly liberated, effectively liberated!

DIRECTOR: *Worthy applauding women, good women of the Great Avant-Garde Party—go for it, go for it in chorus with all your hearts, break the applause meter in your silky robes, with your fabulous smiles and your unbelievable headdresses! You're the symbol of the Party and Nation's dynamism and success! So applaud!*

MINISTER OF THE TERRITORIAL ADMINISTRATION: You women are the lucky ones, because you're the queens! It's only a matter of occupying the empty throne in every man's house —and you'll be queen...

TV ANCHORWOMAN: Of the hearth, dear sisters...

DIRECTOR: *So applaud, my dears!*

MINISTER OF THE INTERIOR: Honestly, dear Sisters, I often say that the real Minister of the Interior is you...

DIRECTOR: *Applaud.*

TV ANCHORWOMAN: After those comforting words, the Empress of Song, our sublime Nzékéba Koné, will calm our last worries with her honey voice, singing her hit number, "Anae," and reminding us just how important motherhood is...

DIRECTOR: *The images on your TV screen dance before you, Londè, and you float between sleep and wakefulness. While the sound grows louder, the singer is absorbed in her performance, stressing her message with those famous gestures you hate so much, gestures which predictably transform her into a mare in heat, a stuffed doll covered with magic charms— charms which become snakes grabbing you by the throat. You wake with a start, screaming in disgust and fear.... You can't take it any more. You stop the program as she shakes her hips in a Mayombe dance.*[3]

---

[3]The Mayombe is a sensual and imploring Zairian dance, which emphasizes movement of the buttocks and hands. (T.N.)

REACTION 1

LONDE: That's enough! Televised nightmares, boredom, and despair! Fizzling and deadening banalities! Insipid women's programs! Enough!

DIRECTOR: *Drop the remote control in your chair now and circle your living room, going again and again from door to door, enraged, like an animal in a cage. You start to open each door but quickly stop yourself, getting angrier and angrier. You study the living room and, finally, you explode:*

LONDE: A home of closets, cupboards, stoves and freezers, a prison home! Cold bedrooms! Is this why I got married?

DIRECTOR: *You jump up and down several times on the seat of your armchair, as if on a spring mattress. Bouncing, you scold the empty armchair facing you.*

LONDE: Behind the pretense of a respectable home, there was just hot air! Would this armchair be any less pumped up if I'd bought it when I was single, with my own money from my job at court? Hot air! Bullshit! Queen of the hearth.... Here I'm dying of loneliness, boredom, and bitterness, in front of a TV lie which shoots craziness directly into the bloodstream!

DIRECTOR: *The mirror projects a pitiful image: a fury with hair on end! What mockery! You burst out... laughing.*

LONDE: But who really stuck me here?

DIRECTOR: *Alas, your laughter was fake; it gets caught in your throat. You need to feel sorry for yourself.... On the brink of tears, you collapse on the armchair, but get up immediately. No, you can't afford to drowse and face those nightmares again. You glance at your watch....*

LONDE: Three days already! Three days in this living room, not daring to open a single other door of my home—not my bedroom door, my husband's, nor our children's.... Doors of fear and pain, doors of unspeakable isolation! Three days in a living room, my God...

DIRECTOR: *Once again you walk around the furniture, touching things, studying them... Let's try to be positive about this, all the same! After all, it is your house, your furniture! And you did struggle to have it all.*

LONDE: But when you think about it, this living room is respectable! It's proof of a couple's success: the weight of the furniture translates the heft of our bank account; and the shine on the knick-knacks suggests the brilliance of future plans. If any guest remains skeptical, she can spill some sauce on her skirt and check out the bathroom: "Oh what a beautiful sink you have! And what fun you must have in that black-flowered bathtub!" She notes the labels of the body lotions, the perfumes, and the shaving cream, and there's no doubt about it: "This couple's a success, it's a real home!" And we so wanted people to believe it. How many guests did we happily direct to the bathroom! And now here I am alone, caught in a trap, a prisoner...

DIRECTOR: *Are you going to fall apart? Burst into tears? But over what and for whom? Who'd feel sorry for you? There's nobody... Only closed doors which mock you! This can't go on. You set off for battle! You decide to enter, but, unfortunately, the door is locked! You panic...*

LONDE: The keys, my God, where are the keys? As soon as I heard the news, I locked everything. But where did I put the keys?

DIRECTOR: *You feverishly search everywhere; finally, you find them behind the television set. As you straighten up, you are again stopped by the photo of your husband which you had turned face down... When? Now you pat it tenderly; you hug it to your breast and speak to it...*

LONDE: How I longed to run to you, to tell you: "Dylemma, my husband, I love you; I've never loved anyone but you." But each time, I was stopped by that door and the hurt it represented. Now that you're gone forever, I want to tell you that you deserved everything we so stupidly messed up! Can you hear me in the other world? Alas, the doors seem closed there too! How often

I called out in vain during those nine months of widowhood. With their jealousy and greed, your brothers almost made me feel like I was being punished. During the whole time they plotted to disinherit me! But you don't disinherit a court officer as easily as an illiterate. They knocked themselves out making me go through the worst, calling it "tradition." And your old grandmother, angry with me for surviving, silently approved.... I accepted everything, hoping you'd send me a sign, a voice, a ghost, at least in a dream. Alas! Only this chilly portrait.

DIRECTOR: *You put the photo back in place and nervously play with the keys.*

LONDE: Now I'm both afraid and ashamed of letting myself into the intimacy we denied each other! If only our children were here! But you enrolled them in a foreign school too far away, as if to protect them from having to see you die.... But I must go in, and face whatever grew in that solitary den where you took refuge. I'm prepared to receive it like a posthumous child left in my belly, to give birth to a symbolic extension of yourself, no matter how painful...

ACTION 2

DIRECTOR: *But why are you trembling so hard as you walk into your husband's bedroom, Londè? After all, it isn't a holy sanctuary! Get a hold of yourself and turn on the lights... Lights on an unknown world, music and images of a man's world: photos of women, strange books, scattered credit cards seem to signal an autonomous existence. Your husband is seated there, with his ear-phones on, savoring the music, filling his life with myriad small delighted gestures, the graphic proof of a life without you... shadows, silhouettes, lights.... In the midst of this you discover with surprise a letter addressed to you. Indeed your name is written in thick red characters on the envelope: to Madame Londè Dylemma. Trembling, you open it and read:*

LONDE: Dearest Londè, my own Wedding Band, my dear, dear wife! When you open this letter, I'll no longer be among the living...

DIRECTOR: *You stagger out of the bedroom in disbelief and shock. Anger overwhelms you; this is the blackness into which everything ought to dis-appear, like a nightmare at the moment of waking. Alas, when day breaks, the letter is still there, in your hands; and anger's in your mind, and pain's in your heart...*

REACTION 2

LONDE: Oh the bastard! So you knew all along.... But since when? Is there a date?

DIRECTOR: *You find the date at the end of the letter, do some rapid calculations and gasp...*

LONDE: It's absurd! How is it possible? Three months before your death? And not one single word out of your mouth? You preferred writing alone in your den? It's monstrous!!!

DIRECTOR: *You crumple the letter and stamp on it in rage ! Then you quickly pick it back up and carefully smooth it, as you would an old parchment containing precious information. You spread it out on the table. And now it's really your husband's voice you hear, calm, a little soft, a little distant—like those times when, suddenly overwhelmed by remorse, his own anger started to drain away...*

HUSBAND: (*off*) Yes, no longer among the living, because I know now, you won't change your mind, you won't ever again enter our marriage bed, and I've already decided not to force the issue another time. Now more than ever, I wouldn't dare!

DIRECTOR: *You slide off your armchair, Londè, and crawl towards your husband's which will forever be empty. As you used to, you curl up against him, your feet tracing his body, his muscles.... Desire overwhelms you for the first time in months....*

LONDE: And I miss them horribly, my husband, those nights when you wanted me so much you overcame all barriers to throw yourself into my arms, crazy with desire! You squeezed my belly, my breasts! You nibbled my ears, my neck... You threatened to slit my wrists if I didn't swear to love you forever, if I didn't tell you nine times over that you were the only man in my life, if I didn't consign to oblivion all those who'd preceded you! Nine times nine I would have sworn anything to you if you hadn't smothered all the sounds emerging from my throat! You made me come the way I think a hanged man releases his last living juices, and you fell with me into a bottomless death... The silence was so beautiful! Everything was said in our souls with such clarity! Alas, your awful suspicions were always revived even before our bodies awoke! Doubts, wounds, venom, and rage. Words which separate, gestures which distance... One day we go too far, and it's too late to undo what's been done! So we say: "I'll never dare again!"

HUSBAND: (*off*) After yesterday's visit to the hospital, I realized it was all over. The diarrhea won't stop, as if my body had experienced a violent desire to rid itself of the excesses of these last years. Excesses of all kinds: tainted relationships, corruption, frustration, hushed-up political manoeuverings, the decay of all my values and hopes. A suffocating body purged of all its stimulating impatience and useless stimulants... Doctor Binam avoided looking me in the face. He said: "We'll do everything we can, but you'll have to be brave. It's viral, you know..."

LONDE: Viral? What do you mean viral? The doctor told me it was a bad case of malaria; and he told you it was a virus? What virus?

HUSBAND: (*off*) When did I get it?

LONDE: He's asking me that question? Oh my God, all his hair falling out in record time! And his skin peeling like an onion's? I was so afraid to think it might be...

HUSBAND: (*off*) Could I have given it to you?

LONDE: What? Me? Never! It's been years since we've slept together.

DIRECTOR: *Are you so sure? If so, why the nervousness which makes you clutch your hands together and bite your lips? Why are you trembling so hard you're about to fall over?*

LONDE: Contaminated? Without knowing it? My God!

HUSBAND: (*off*) And what about the children?

LONDE: Have you gone crazy, too? How could our children have anything to do with this?

HUSBAND: (*off*) Because—if you're the one who brought home this virus—given the life you've led ...

LONDE: Oh come on! Here we go again! Dylemma, my husband, doubts will hound you 'till the grave! And in the end you show such a lack of trust that I no longer know who I was during those first twenty-three years, before you barged into my life. And even less during the twelve years we spent together until you abandoned me for good on the edge of death...or is it life? I don't know any more! It's too much! I need a drink! It's really too much!

DIRECTOR: *One drink, one glass! Then another, and yet another, in cadence! To the rhythm of your fall, of your descent into hell. Bending, breaking! Halting steps! Breasts, belly and buttocks shaking. Trance.... Seek help—on automatic pilot—seek help from the last resort, from the television escape machine.... Alas, today, Londè, in your country as in mine, television no longer entertains but stupefies. And your overworked mind transforms every image into something monstrous.... Sleep, that's the answer. Sleep! Escape! God, deliver us from hallucinatory advertisements and TV hostesses whose improbably tiny heads emerge as if by magic from mountains of draped cloth!*

ACTION 3

TV ANCHORWOMAN: Dear sisters, I'm delighted to introduce as today's "Special Guest," Mister Kpalé Digbé, Head of the Psychology Department of the National University. This week he'll speak to us about his research on feminine psychology within the student milieu. Let's hear what he has to say...

DIRECTOR: *We'll listen to him, you bet, with his eunuch's voice, his pontificating finger-jabbing style. Notice his ingratiating but ill-defined gestures, like someone uncomfortable with his sexuality. Sure, let's listen to him...*

HEAD OF PSYCHOLOGY DEPARTMENT: We have discovered without a doubt that the female student between the ages of eighteen and twenty-three suffers from a complex which we've come to call "the schizoid-libidinal syndrome." On the one hand, her sensitivity and sexuality, newly awakened by adolescence, impels her to devote herself...

TV ANCHORWOMAN: To what?

HEAD OF PSYCHOLOGY DEPARTMENT: To a man, of course, to a home, to children, naturally...

TV ANCHORWOMAN: And not to creative activities or conceptualizations, as one would expect of any intellectual, young or old?

HEAD OF PSYCHOLOGY DEPARTMENT: That's just it, it's that intellect, precociously developed through education and meant to exalt the male ego and prepare it for power, that puts too much pressure on the female student's natural generosity, either repressing her desires or perverting them into a false notion of freedom which is even more frustrating for her libido...

TV ANCHORWOMAN: Nevertheless, the young male student experiences the same sensual awakening, the same desires, and that doesn't keep him from developing his intellect!

HEAD OF PSYCHOLOGY DEPARTMENT: What's needed is a

strength and buoyancy which women do not have, a calm which they often lose, planning and distancing at moments when women tend to forget themselves and hang on. The man, who is naturally unfaithful, has no difficulty pursuing all manner of simultaneous activities. That's exactly where the woman feels torn apart... It's this typically female condition of being pulled in too many directions at once that we've come to call...

TV ANCHORWOMAN: The schizoid-libidinal syndrome! Dear Sisters, remember this lesson when your daughters become students, and pray that by then we'll have found a vaccine against the virus which sets the syndrome in motion...

DIRECTOR: *The fingers of the Professor and the TV Anchorwoman appear to you now like giant caterpillars seeking each other out, coupling, and multiplying into countless viruses. Are men and women no more than anthropomorphic viruses? In your light sleep, Londè, you're exceedingly agitated! You're delirious...*

LONDE: Viruses, syndromes.... Trendy new words! So everything becomes a virus, a syndrome, even the television dilemma infecting us! Turning it on means shooting up with polluted images and dying of mindlessness! Turning it off means facing solitude, the knowledge of all those advanced syndromes, and dying of fear, the worst virus of all.... What should I do?

DIRECTOR: *Turn it off, just the same! The show's over! All that's left is static. That's it.... But why are you covering your ears? What's still blasting so unbearably?*

HUSBAND: (*off*) Because, if you're the one who brought the virus home, given the life you've led...

LONDE: You mean given the life you forced us to lead: a life of doubt and endless suspicion, a living hell! How I envy your eternal sleep in death's shadows, where memories are wiped away! I hope the virus does carry me off, so the searchlights in my head, in my heart, and under my skin go dead! Give me black night, dear God, please!!!

REACTION 3

DIRECTOR: *Night engulfs you like an abyss. You're floating like a twig on an expanse of crooked and rebellious memories which won't let go. You're floating.... A privileged spectator, you see through a scrim a scene from your past.... Lit from the side, your husband's silhouette walks nervously across the screen. You see yourself move towards him, happy, victorious. On the way, you pour out two glasses of something bubbly. You move towards your husband, gayer still, pirouetting and dancing around him, already high...*

LONDE: Come, my love, let's drink to your success, to our future. I've finally got official permission for your project, nearly had to turn myself inside out! You can be proud of me, we've won!

DIRECTOR: *Alas, he violently shoves you away and, your breath knocked out of you, you stammer something in reply; you don't even remember what! But you still hear, as though you were there, his extraordinarily aggressive voice clearly regretting the last-minute gesture he made to catch you. After realizing you have miraculously managed to stay on your feet and not break your head open, he yells:*

HUSBAND: (*off*) Leave me alone and take that permit back to the Minister, your lover ! I don't want it any more!!!

DIRECTOR: *Hypocrisy or injustice? Miscommunication for sure! Casting judgment so far from the truth can't be called anything else! But how can miscommunication be so frequent and so enormous between people who say they love each other? No, in fact, it must be hypocrisy. This proves it.... Your answer is nearly a stutter!*

LONDE: Another lover? You're unbelievable...and...you don't want the permit any more? But ...for months, right up 'till now, you've been after me to try and unblock it, insisting that your career and our entire future depended on it.... And all of a sudden, you don't want it any more?

HUSBAND: (*off*) I don't want to owe anything to your ex-lovers!

LONDE: What the hell are you talking about? You bastard! You waited until I got this stinking paper before deciding to get smart with me? Did your spy network just discover this new "ex-lover?"

HUSBAND: (*off*) How dare you talk back to me? Tell me, how many lovers did you have before finding the idiot who married you, thinking he was committing himself to a decent young student, the future mother of his children?

LONDE: And didn't I give you children? Since only decent women can do that, I must be one!

HUSBAND: (*off*) How many, I'm asking you! How many lovers? Ten, twenty, a hundred? Can you even count them?

LONDE: And what if we tried counting your mistresses? Let's not bother with the ones before you trapped the naive student who thought she'd found her very own man and not a social worker! Sure, let's not bother with them; but let's count the ones after: the fragile, silent one who grabbed hold so tight and so well that you took pity on her, the childhood friend in trouble, the titillating out-of-town client who threw herself at you, your uncles' widows whom tradition required you to console.... All those affairs which, of course, don't really matter in a man's life, as long as he doesn't leave his wife.... Can you count them?

HUSBAND: (*off*) Women as shameless as you are rare in this world! But how could you have learned to respect a husband, raised as you were by a single mother?

LONDE: Since my father fled his responsibilities, I guess there was no way I could have! Naturally, every woman should learn to respect her husband, even if he's nothing but a coward and a crook.

HUSBAND: (*off*) A coward because he ran away from a loose woman, because he hadn't wanted to father her children?

LONDE: Loose... a woman who took complete responsibility for herself, who made sure her daughter had a real home, filled with mother love, who taught her to make her way in life on her own with courage and dignity? So as not to be held in contempt, I suppose she should have spent her whole life chasing after the respectable status of married woman, like your mother, even if that meant three divorces and two dead husbands!

HUSBAND: (*off*) In any event, my mother was always a lady; everyone respected her! I forbid you to insinuate anything about her past!

LONDE: She didn't die from my "insinuations," but from the rough treatment and venereal diseases inflicted by her honorable husbands!

HUSBAND: (*off*) I'm warning you, stop talking about the dead! There's plenty to be said about your own mother who hangs on to life like an octopus, stockpiling wealth and buying herself the respectability her daughter got for free by trapping a prize husband whom she doesn't even respect!

LONDE: Listen, if my mother's money bothers you so much, you can just stop using it to parade in front of your girlfriends and your proud-as-peacock buddies! And then you have the nerve to complain about it.... If you're so uncomfortable with yourself, do something about it; but don't try to get under my skin. I won't stand for it!

HUSBAND: (*off*) Oh yes you will! I want to get under your skin! That's exactly what I want. I want to make you feel bad, real bad! Damn it, I'm your husband!

DIRECTOR: *War broke out among the giraffes. It left its marks! Between remembrance and reality, between being there and shadow. Your husband's silhouette engulfs your own, Londè. You hear the sound of the slaps he directs towards you, one after the other.... Shaken, you see him tear off your robe, hug you to him, excite you. You feel him pull all your repressed desires from the depths of your determination.*
On the scrim, your husband's presence is sometimes a graphic design

hovering over you, dissolving and disappearing into your shadow, some-
times a silhouette teasing you into a combat of silky cloth and fully fleshed-
out gestures.... A phantasy of the husband-lover, always dreamed, always
fleeing! A fight? No! A dance... A loving dance, an erotic dance, to a
background music of heavy breathing. Dance, peak, roll...building
waves and breaking waves! Desire....
Londè, there you are swept away into an empty space, like a buoy on a
deserted beach.... The tide of memories has ebbed: we can hear the snores
of your contented husband.... You shake him gently...

LONDE: Don't fall asleep, my love. Don't go away, please. Don't
leave me again. I'm going to explain the "before you" which
hurt you so...listen....
My heart is like the universe.
There's a place for everything and everyone.
No one can take anyone else's place.
There's a place for friendship. And for admiration.
There's a drive towards passion. And another towards reason.
There's desire for the touch of skin. And desire for games of
the spirit.
The need for simple affection. And the dream of creativity.
My mother told me: "These are men's ambitions, a woman does-
n't have the right; a woman is made for a single love!"
If so, then what am I?
How can one explain the multitude of feelings, the rich emo-
tional palette of my soul?
Each new face is a new planet.
Each new meeting a new storm which carries me towards a
new quest.
I've ridden a new desire each day hitched up to a new star.
But how many hopes have been crushed by careless hands that
squeeze you like mangoes on display?
How much desire wrecked on the shores of triviality by mouths
compelled to insult and humiliate in order to create illusions
of power and pleasure?
Before you, I fled sexual fulfillment to love only its promise—
When all the creative forces pour out of the body like a primal fire
Ardently streaming towards infinite skies.
For fulfillment is the death of desire

The fall of vitality
The sublime trip's end
The beginning of sleep
And the snores which mean forgetfulness.

DIRECTOR: *You get up and slip on a maternity dress while the englobing percussive music modulates and begins to build like a wave, or an ancient lullaby. Your tender song accompanies it. Your husband's breathing swells it. The squealing of little children adds to it. It's the lament of the conjugal swamp, of routines which have relegated duty-bound marriages to a rut.*

LONDE: I forgave even your snoring, my husband,
In order to imagine a safe haven.
I discovered the feelings of belonging, of property
The kind of security and rights that lawfulness gives you.
Is this what they call "conjugal love?"
All this because I loved you then. And I was faithful to you. I know you know it!
Yes. I think I loved you.
For if it wasn't love, what can make a woman stand a man's snores?
A man who starts life moving in her belly
Then falls asleep, peacefully...
And while she swells, he snores!
Yes, I think I loved you.
I had such hopes of sharing eternity with you!
To give you a child, multiply and prolong you.
Your snoring even partook of the breath of life, its vital force...
Alas, marriage is what it is.
The experience of a lifetime is transformed into habit
Into social constraints.
Families get involved
And the married couple becomes, at best, marionettes for perpetuating tradition.

DIRECTOR: *The music is becoming too oppressive, the ambience too imprisoning, and you move more and more like a zombie! Don't fade*

away. Hang on! Look, you're walking on something... the letter! A let-
ter you've read and re-read many times but which remains strange, impos-
sible to understand.... How could you have miscommunicated like that?
What lack of clarity! What inaccuracy!

HUSBAND: (*off*) No, I'm not in pain, but rather afraid. A thousand and one fears torture me.... The fear of seeming ugly,
useless, the same fear which walled us up in our individual soli-
tudes, when according to the marriage contract we should have
been one...

LONDE: One and undivided, what a joke! How many people
don't give a damn about themselves, smashing and destroying
their own lives but still being able to take on the impossible to
please a person they admire, often someone inaccessible, someone other than themselves, "the other," the ideal.... If a husband
or wife remained the ideal and didn't suddenly become by
official decree a part of oneself, the "taken-for-granted part,"
which gets treated any which way, we'd always be careful, and it
would be wonderful...

HUSBAND: (*off*) I'm also afraid of the solitude waiting for you
when I'll no longer be there to goad you. You, my driving force,
my myriad inspirations! But I console myself by thinking: our
couple has fulfilled its mission. Our children will grow up free
of need. You can even re-marry. But why would you? You're so
free, so independent.... You hold the key to your own desires
and the secret of your own pleasure. Will you still need a husband? Did you ever need me?

LONDE: I needed you terribly, your gaze, your hands... I needed
your need for me; it gave me a reason to live...

HUSBAND: (*off*) I don't believe it and that's why I was so uncomfortable with myself! A woman as complete as you makes a
man useless, becomes a way of negating him! But since I loved
and admired you, if I'd had the least notion of being useful,
I'd have fought heaven and hell...

DIRECTOR: *How do you accept that you've suffered from the same absence, that while living together you each hoarded the love the other needed and withered away from loneliness and misunderstanding? It's enough to enrage you!!! How frustrating can life get?*

LONDE: One has to have at least one certainty in order to live! But you, you lived only on doubt! You married doubt, and I merely summoned and nourished it. What a hard role you gave me, Dylemma, my husband!

HUSBAND: (*off*) When you find this letter, I'll no longer be alive. But I'm writing it while I still can, in order to express to you in no uncertain terms all the love I never really knew how to prove. I hope you'll find here, even if posthumously, everything you've always wanted from me, and that it will be as crucial to you as you have always been to me.... But I'm probably worrying over nothing, you'll have everything you need, you won't need anyone! In the worst of cases, you'll have amorous adventures, a "merry" widow...

DIRECTOR: *Should you laugh? Cry? Cry and laugh! Impotent tears in the face of what can never be fixed. There's no worse failure than one that can't be justified.... What are you going to do now? Try at least to be successful in your career and live out the freedom you've paid for so dearly? Start all over again from nothing and re-learn how to share? But what's making you laugh?*

LONDE: A widow...probably forever! I've lost my certainty. I've caught the virus of doubt. A widow forever? I guess I've no other choice! "Merry?" What for?

DIRECTOR: *Why not? Because experience broadens our consciousness. Because life goes on. Because there's pleasure in sharing. Look, on the television you've just turned on through force of habit, they're showing* A Tuareg Gets Married to a Pygmy,[4] *the last*

---

[4]This play, written by Werewere Liking, was produced by Liking's Ki-Yi Theatre in 1992-1993. (T.N.)

theatre piece you saw together and liked so much.... There's that last image of water surging forth, and the polyphonic voices.... How can you resist such a call to life? Why not end on a positive note? While the credits roll at the end of the program, you begin a song of hope, hold out your hands to a wide-open future, and disappear into your bedroom from where you can finally begin life anew...

~

MARYSE CONDE

THE TROPICAL BREEZE HOTEL

Translated from the French by

BARBARA BREWSTER LEWIS

CATHERINE TEMERSON

UBU REPERTORY THEATER PUBLICATIONS
NEW YORK

Maryse Condé was born on the island of Guadeloupe in the French West Indies and she received her doctorate at the Sorbonne in Paris. Though well known as a fiction writer, Condé began her literary career writing for the stage and has authored five plays, among them *The Hills of Massabielle* produced by Ubu Repertory Theater in 1991. Condé's novels include the best seller *Segu* published by Ballantine Press (1990), *A Season in Rihata* (1980), *I, Tituba, Black Witch of Salem* (1993), *The Children of Segu* (1991), and *Tree of Life* (1992). She is also the author of a collection of Francophone Caribbean folktales and several works of criticism. Ms. Condé is the recipient of a Guggenheim Fellowship, the prestigious French award Le Grand Prix Littéraire de la Femme, and the coveted prix de l'Académie Française for her novel *La Vie scélérate* (1987). She has taught West Indian literature at the Sorbonne and has lectured widely in the United States. Ms. Condé teaches at the University of Maryland and at the University of Virginia. She currently lives in Washington, D.C.

Barbara Brewster Lewis teaches theater at City College and writing at New York University. Her work has appeared in *Fiction*, the *African American Review*, the *Amsterdam News*, *Essence*, *Ms. Magazine*, *The Kenyon Review* and *Black Women in America: An Historical Encyclopedia*.

Catherine Temerson's previous translations include short stories, essays, film and radio scripts. She translated Jean-Claude Grumberg's *The Free Zone* and *The Workroom*, and co-translated Simone Schwarz-Bart's *Your Handsome Captain* and Denise Chalem's *The Sea Between Us*, all published by Ubu Repertory Theater .

The Tropical Breeze Hotel, in Barbara Brewster Lewis and Catherine Temerson's translation, had its first staged reading at Ubu Repertory Theater, 15 West 28th Street, New York, NY 10001, on April 11th, 1994.

AUTHOR'S NOTE

Very young, I was attracted to the theater. Olga, the neighbors' maid, used to masquerade and go running about the streets of Pointe à Pitre during carnival. Weekdays I would see her go off to market, gentle and quiet, a basket in hand. Sunday afternoons, she popped out of the hallway of her employers' house, wearing dried banana leaves or, at other times, blackened with thick tar and cracking a whip, or again, crowned with horns and dressed in jute, her face always hidden behind a mask. Was she the same person? I was terrified as I witnessed these varied transformations. To me, they were magical metamorphoses.

When I was six or seven, I tried my hand at dramatic writing. For my mother's birthday I wrote a play, in verse I think, my childish imagination representing her as I saw her, as a supreme goddess who made all her worshippers—my father, my brothers, my sisters and I—bow our heads in her presence. Predictably, she didn't like the piece, which revealed a truth to me: people are rarely pleased with the image we have of them.

As an adolescent, and later as a student in Paris, I gorged myself on theater. Anything would do: comedy, tragedy, vaudeville. But only once, at the Odéon, did I experience the feelings Olga had inspired during carnival. I attended a performance of Jean Genet's *The Blacks*. The director was Roger Blin. The actors—Bachir Touré, Toto Bissainthe, Judith Aucaguos, Mamadou Condé—wore masks doubly concealing their identity.

During the years I lived in Africa, I learned to admire other artistic forms. I discovered a traditional art that could compete with the modern forms I had seen in France. However, as I was inhibited by my childhood experience, I only ventured to write for the stage years later: serious plays, dramas, indeed you might say tragedies, because, at the time, I was influenced by a certain kind of politically committed literature and would never have dared break out of the mold even if I had felt cramped. *Dieu nous l'a donné* was performed during the 1973 Theater Festival of Fort de France, directed by Ivan Labejoff; *Mort d'Oluwemi d'Ajumako,* at the Blaise Senghor Cultural Center in Dakar by the Théâtre du Toucan.

I only managed to free myself from this pattern with *Pension les Alizés (The Tropical Breeze Hotel)*, a sentimental comedy, part light entertainment, which I wrote for my friend Sonia Emmanuel. The character of the talented black actress who is denied a part and forced to silence her temperament fascinated me at once. It is the inspiration behind *La Colonie du Nouveau Monde,* which my readers reproachfully tell me is my saddest novel. Sonia, for me, incarnated the all too rare qualities of intelligence, will power, and a sort of disenchanted lucidity. As a way of exorcising the future, I projected her into this character of an aging beauty who is without bitterness but completely ravaged; she created the role, with great success, at the Center for the Arts in Pointe à Pitre in March, 1988, and performed it again several months later in Martinique. Together we dreamed of landmark performances, and of instituting a repertoire for West Indian and African actresses. We were certainly overly ambitious.

Today, however, Emma is romanticizing her past in English, in New York. So perhaps our dream has begun to take root after all?

MARYSE CONDE

For Sonia

CHARACTERS

EMMA

ISHMAEL

FIRST TABLEAU

SCENE 1

Interior of a middle-class Parisian apartment: expensive-looking furniture and a thousand and one knickknacks. A large portrait of a woman of about thirty, possibly younger, dominates one wall; she is wearing bulky jewelry and looks like a woman of questionable virtue. There are bookshelves full of books. The overall impression is one of filth and slovenliness. The light is dim. Emma is slowly making herself up as she sits in front of a mirror. She is beautiful but very weary.

EMMA: Only a little bit more! Now, that's fine! When I'd stick on my false eyelashes, that's when the show would begin! (*She turns around, stands, and wraps a rather shapeless dress around her. She bows several times as if an invisible crowd were giving her an ovation.*) Thank you! Thank you! The new Josephine Baker, that's what they used to call me! But I never really liked being called that! When I saw it in the papers, I was mad. Because I refused to wear a belt of bananas. I was a dignified black woman ... dignified. Yes, dignified! I was one beautiful black woman! A real beauty! Like the song said, I had teeth like pearls. (*She hums to herself.*) And such skin! When I was little, Mama would kiss me and say, "What pretty skin you have. As smooth as a plum." And when her friends would come over to the house for some sherbet, they would all fondle me and say. "She has such pretty skin! Just like a plum!" (*Pause.*) I never saw Mama's grave. They wrote me and told me she had a beautiful funeral. The school children were all dressed in white. There were flowers everywhere, flowers and wreaths. Half the people in Pointe-à-Pitre marched behind her casket. But I wasn't there. (*Pause.*) Come now, all that's over and done with. You shouldn't brood over the past. Over things in the past that were painful. It's like thinking about teeth being pulled out. I had a wisdom tooth extracted once, boy was it painful! My mouth was full of blood! I couldn't eat for weeks. No, one shouldn't brood over things like that ... The new Josephine Baker! Now that's much more pleasant! (*She begins her routine again. Bows.*) When I started, they asked me to change my name. "Emma Boisgris is too common," they said. I refused. I was born Emma Boisgris and Emma Boisgris I'll stay. Boisgris. It seems that there was a runaway slave in our family, a marron with that name. An ancestor. That's what Papa used to say. Some story! A marron, you bet! So, of course, Papa was furious when I started to dance. "That child is bringing dishonor to our name!" He didn't understand. He couldn't. Those were dark days, as dark as the blackboard in a classroom. Everyone was on rations. Meat was an unattainable luxury! Who could study? I think it was God, God himself, who sent Guido to me. "My dear, with your looks, you could have Paris at your feet!" And Paris couldn't grovel fast enough. (*She laughs.*) They bowed. Men were bowed down in front of me like sugar cane swaying in the breeze. All races. All colors. There was this American: "After Paris, I'll take you to New York and you can take Broadway by storm.... But I was afraid and didn't go. I don't like Americans. I don't like their way of talking. My dressing room was always full to the brim with flowers. "Exotic and fiery just like you." That's what they used to say! You bet! I never fell for that kind of talk. I was a dignified black woman. Level-headed. (*Pause.*) I was born in Marie-Galante, in the La Treille neighborhood. Yes, that's where I was born, in Marie-Galante, a prophetic birthplace considering what I would become: a woman who attracts gallantries! Funny, isn't it? I was seven or eight when the family moved to Pointe-à-Pitre. We moved to a little house, tucked between a garden and a courtyard, in the hills of Massabielle. There was an Indian tamarind tree in the garden. Mama made jam from the fruit. Yes, I was born in Marie-Galante, in La Treille. Papa and Mama weren't just anybody. Papa was a male nurse. People would come and wake him in the middle of the night. "Rodrigo Boisgris, *pitite an-mwen ka mo*, my child is dying!" He would get up out of bed and get his bag. He's the one who wanted me to become a doctor. But in those days who could set their mind on studying? I had to climb seven flights to a freezing maid's room. I used to sell my landlord the coffee Mama sent. The family would drink it right in front of me without offering me a cup! Things like that show you how selfish some people are! When I was hired at the New Venus, I sent them an invitation so they could see what had become of me. You think they might have thanked me? No, I doubt they even bothered to come. For people like that, going to a neighborhood like Pigalle is like taking a trip to hell! (*The doorbell rings. Emma doesn't move. There's another, much louder ring. A man enters. He is young and dressed like an immigrant worker, though he looks like an intellectual. He is carrying a suitcase.*) Who are you? What do you want?

ISHMAEL: The door was open. So I came in. I'm Max's friend.

EMMA: Max's friend? How? What day is it? Oh my God, I forgot. I was all wrapped up in my thoughts. Come in. Make yourself at home. You can sleep right here. My bedroom is over there. The kitchen and bathroom are at the end of the hall. You want something to drink? Coffee? Rum? Punch? Yes, how about punch? I bought a lime yesterday and I have some cane sugar. The weather is supposed to be dreadful, unfit for a dog. That's according to the weather broadcast, I haven't been out yet. What time is it?

ISHMAEL: Ten twenty. Sure, I'd love some punch. But only if it isn't too much trouble.

EMMA: Not at all! I'll have some with you. I never drink alone. But it's different if I have company. (*She disappears for a few seconds. Left alone, Ishmael puts his suitcase down, then stands in front of the portrait on the wall, examining it. Emma comes back. She busies herself with serving the drinks.*) This rum is from Marie-Galante. It's the best. 59 proof. It's not easy to find. It can be used to flambé cakes, crêpes Suzette...

ISHMAEL: Crêpes Suzette?

EMMA: Yes. You've never eaten any? Mama used to make them all the time and this is the only rum she used. Do you know Guadeloupe? Have you been there?

ISHMAEL: Know it? I was there once.

Emma fills the glasses. Ishmael empties his quickly.

EMMA: I heard there are no more tamarind trees on the hills of Massabielle. Is that true? They tell me they leveled Miquel Hill, and that Place de la Victoire is now a parking lot and lovers don't meet there any more.

ISHMAEL: I don't know. I only stayed a few days and besides ... I was there for a conference. We didn't do any sightseeing!

EMMA: I heard you could walk all over town and not see a single tree, not one breadfruit or flame tree. There's concrete everywhere.

Ishmael pours himself a second glass of rum and drains it dry.

ISHMAEL: It was very cold outside and I waited several hours for Max before deciding to come here. Do you know where he is?

EMMA: Who? Max? No. Who are you? First of all, what's your name?

ISHMAEL: Call me Ishmael.

EMMA: Ishmael? What kind of name is that? Where are you from?

ISHMAEL: I'm Haitian.

EMMA: I knew a man from Haiti once. He was an ambassador and he used to invite me to his home. I never knew a man who spoke French like he did. He told me...

ISHMAEL: Well, as for me... I'm the opposite of an ambassador.

EMMA: You're not into drug dealing, are you?

ISHMAEL: Drug dealing?

EMMA: You never know with Max's friends. But where is he?

ISHMAEL: That's what I just asked you! He was supposed to meet me at the train station, but he never showed up. Luckily, he had already given me your address. I asked people how to get here. I walked. That's why I'm so cold.

EMMA: Max is the son of a man who loved me very much.

ISHMAEL: He never mentioned his father. Actually, I don't know him very well. We met at some conferences and when he said he could help me...

EMMA: To do what?

ISHMAEL: To find work.

EMMA: I suppose you've heard that there's a worldwide recession? Even white people are lining up at the Salvation Army.... What are your skills, anyway?

ISHMAEL: I was a physician at home.

EMMA: A physician? Oh, that's different. Physicians are never unemployed.

ISHMAEL: Not a physician like me. With no papers, no residence permit. I'm worth no more than the man who cleans the street.

EMMA: Don't go looking down your nose at street cleaners... it's not a bad job.

ISHMAEL: I didn't say it was. But cleaning streets is not my profession.

EMMA: Maybe that's not what you said, but that's what you were thinking! I know your kind, you have minds as narrow as match sticks. "Their daughter...yes...the oldest one, the one who went away to study medicine." Medicine, yes, me too. "She dances nude in a cabaret in Pigalle." " A nude dancer?" " Yes, my dear, she shows her ass off to the whites!" You know what life was like then? The cold, the hunger, the rationing. They withdrew my scholarship the first year. So what did anyone expect me to do?

ISHMAEL: I didn't expect anything, Ma'am. Don't get all worked up.

EMMA: (*imitating him*) Don't get all worked up. I don't know you from Adam, I take you in, and already you're insulting me?

ISHMAEL: I'm insulting you? How?

EMMA: Spit it out. Say what's on your mind. You think I'm a whore?

ISHMAEL: A whore? What's a whore?

EMMA: Oh, no, please. Spare me your philosophizing. You know perfectly well what I mean. Say it! Say what you're thinking!

ISHMAEL: (*very weary*) Believe me, I'm not thinking anything. All I want is a roof over my head and a place to stretch out. Didn't you say I could bed down here?

EMMA: (*in tears*) A whore! A whore!

ISHMAEL: Please, Ma'am. Don't get all worked up!

EMMA: Ma'am? Don't Ma'am me. My name is Emma!

SCENE 2

The stage is dark. A sofa bed is open and someone is stretched out on it. Suddenly, the person jumps up and utters several piercing cries. The door opens. Emma enters, dressed in a rather luxurious nightgown. She turns on the light and runs toward Ishmael.

EMMA: What's wrong?

ISHMAEL: No! No! No!

EMMA: But what's wrong?

Ishmael wakes up and looks around. He gets up. He is practically naked.

EMMA: Put some clothes on! A woman my age has no business looking at naked men.

He obeys, speaking in very low tones as he gets dressed.

ISHMAEL: Forgive me! I was having a nightmare. I've always had nightmares. When I was little, I used to think there was a crab hidden inside my bed waiting to bite me.

EMMA: Yeah. And what were you having a nightmare about just now?

ISHMAEL: It's always the same recurrent one! I was...

EMMA: I'd say that anyone who has nightmares like that must not have a very clear conscience.

ISHMAEL: A clear conscience? Do you know anyone who has a clear conscience? Doesn't everyone have some disgusting little thing they did hidden under the pretty exterior shell of their lives? Like a worm hidden in a fruit. One day I went to visit my godmother. She lived on rue Bois Patate and there was this bowl of shiny red apples on the dining room table. The urge was just too strong. I stole one. I hid it in my pants pocket and as soon as I got outside, crunch! I bit right into it. And I bit into a black worm...

EMMA: Stop it, stop! Don't try to confuse me! You're a doctor. What have you done to end up with no money and no papers, forced to sleep in the apartment of a woman you don't even know?

ISHMAEL: There's no one answer to that question. I'd tell you that I haven't done anything. Others, I'd rather not hear what they'd tell you. It's always the same story. There's no such thing as the truth! One person says white, another says black.

EMMA: You missed your calling. You should've been a lawyer. You're such a fine talker! Is everyone like that in your country? I'm beginning to think so. I told you, the other Haitian I knew was an ambassador.

ISHMAEL: (*screaming*) And I told you already! I'm the opposite of an ambassador! (*He gets hold of himself.*) Forgive me! Do you have any more rum?

She disappears for a moment, then comes back and serves him.

ISHMAEL: (*drinking*) Hum, that's good! I'm not afraid for myself, you understand. I'm afraid for her!

EMMA: Her? Who are you talking about?

ISHMAEL: They haven't done anything to her yet. I called her when I was in New York. She was able to talk to me. Not for a long time though! Still, I found out she wasn't in danger...

EMMA: Okay! I don't understand anything in this mixed up story! But you seem to be feeling better. I'll leave you ...

ISHMAEL: (*rushing over and taking her hand*) No, don't leave me. If I'm alone, if I go back to bed, I'll fall asleep and I'll have nightmares again...

EMMA: You think I'm a nanny? (*She changes her mind and goes toward him.*) I used to have recurrent nightmares too at one time. That was right after my mother's death. It wasn't just that she died. But that she died before I could explain. Papa was wrong about me. I didn't have it in me to become a doctor. First of all, I can't stand the sight of blood! Secondly, I'm not very smart. My brain isn't the best thing about me. I only had a body. And I made it work for me.

ISHMAEL: Listen, if it will make you feel better, tell me about it.

EMMA: Tell you? No, you couldn't possibly understand! As soon as I saw you come in, I knew the kind of person I was dealing with. I can smell the bourgeoisie miles away! They've made my life hard enough! You know how I know them? By their eyes! Their eyes that are always judging. By their mouths. Their mouths made for spitting out gossip and slander.

ISHMAEL: You're mistaken! I don't like the bourgeoisie any more than you do. And I'm not one of them. My father was a shoemaker in Léogane. My mother was a housewife. You know how I was able to get through medical school? Thanks to her.

EMMA: Her again! Who is she?

ISHMAEL: My wife! She fed me and gave me a place to stay! She's the one who bought me cigarettes ...

EMMA: (*getting up*) Great! I've had enough of this! Good night!

> *Ishmael holds her back. She tries to get away and there is a kind of erotic struggle between them.*

ISHMAEL: Stay here with me.

EMMA: Don't get so familiar with me, young man.

ISHMAEL: Stay! I've always been afraid of the night.

EMMA: Don't talk to me that way! I don't feel sorry for you! In the West Indies, all the children are afraid of the night. Mama used to tell me that a monster had swallowed up the sun and that if I said my prayers like a good girl and stopped calling her every two minutes, the sun would come back in the morning shining like a new penny. So I would try very hard to go to sleep.

ISHMAEL: You're always talking about your mother.

EMMA: What's so unusual about that? We only have one mother.

ISHMAEL: Unfortunately!

EMMA: (*horrified*) Unfortunately!

ISHMAEL: (*He gets up.*) I lied to you, Emma. I'm not a shoemaker's son.

EMMA: I knew that right from the start! I had a friend. He was English. He used to say, "You can't take...."

ISHMAEL: My father was one of the biggest wheels in the regime. He sat at the right of Papa Doc presiding over a cemetery. He was in on every killing that took place. And my mother helped him get to the top. She slept in all the right places and fucked all the right people just so her husband could get to the top...

EMMA: How can you talk that way about your mother!

ISHMAEL: You see, you had me pegged as a member of the bourgeoisie. But you're just as conventional as they are. A man should honor and cherish his mother, isn't that right? Well, I hate my mother. It's her fault I'm in the mess I'm in.

EMMA: Stop being so vague. What is it you did back in your own country?

ISHMAEL: Everyone will give you a different version of the facts. What's the point? I don't know when I first wanted to change the world. Wanted it to be right, to be different! But because I was who I was, no one took me seriously. In Mexico City, where I went to study, I tried to spend time with Haitian exiles. But everyone was suspicious of me, "Look out for him, he's the son of so-and-so." I persisted, I wanted to be accepted, I wanted to be trusted. But they were always finding something to hold against me. If it wasn't my family, it was my wife. Because she was white.

EMMA: Oh my God.

ISHMAEL: Later, it was because I earned too much money. What can I do about it? I'm a physician. It's not my fault that people get sick and need medical attention! (*He pours himself a drink.*)

EMMA: I don't like men who drink.

ISHMAEL: My wife isn't very beautiful, but she loves me. You black women don't know how to love a man. You want him to be strong, a male, both in bed and out!... Doesn't it seem strange to you that Max didn't come to meet me? And that he hasn't even called? Can you call him?

EMMA: I don't know where Max lives. He's always so mysterious. Once he called me and hung up right away. He claimed my phone was bugged! Can you imagine! What does he do for a living?

ISHMAEL: I have no idea. I thought you could tell me. I think he teaches somewhere!

EMMA: Pity today's young people! In my day, teachers were responsible individuals. Now they're communists or drug addicts.

ISHMAEL: Bravo! You're really broad-minded!

EMMA: How long are you planning to stay here?

ISHMAEL: At the moment, I don't really know. Max was supposed to help me out and, see, he hasn't even shown up.

EMMA: I'm sure he'll show up tomorrow. I'll tell you something. I hope he comes real soon and takes you with him. I don't particularly like you. You're... there's something fishy about you.

ISHMAEL: You think I'm fishy! That's because I'm not trying to get you into bed. Women always want you to pay court to them. If you're alone with a woman and haven't jumped on top of her after five minutes, you must be impotent... Though, you know, you are a hell of a beautiful woman!

EMMA: You should have seen me when I was twenty!

ISHMAEL: Beautiful women frighten me. I only feel comfortable with women who are a bit ugly, like my wife. (*He goes to pour himself another drink then changes his mind.*) I hope nothing's happened to her! When will we see each other again, I wonder! Maybe never! I'll die here and she'll never know. She won't even know where I'm buried and will never see my grave.

EMMA: That's the hardest part.... Like all Italians, Guido was a believer, and he would try to calm me down: "Up there," he used to say, "she sees and understands everything. I'm sure she's forgiven you." I've got to go back, if only for that: to kneel at her grave! I hope they'll have forgotten and won't still be there whispering: "nude dancer... nude dancer..."

ISHMAEL: Don't worry yourself so! People have short memories.

EMMA: Not where I come from! We're like elephants. Mama used to tell me things that she remembered from her mother and her grandmother. Our memory doesn't need books, or words laid out on sheets of paper. Our memory lives and will never die.

ISHMAEL: What are you saying? I tell you, people forget! They're incredibly fickle! One day people will probably say that this Baby Doc that everyone is trying to overthrow wasn't so bad!

EMMA: It seems that his wife was worse than he was!... Are you mixed up in these stories?

ISHMAEL: What stories?

EMMA: I read the newspapers like everyone else. I watch television. I know what's happening in Haiti.

ISHMAEL (*shouting*): You know nothing! Nothing at all! No one knows anything. There's no one truth...

EMMA: Okay, okay!... No need to shout like that! My God, you must have a lot on your conscience! (*The phone rings suddenly. They stare at it. Then Emma runs to answer it.*) Hello! Max! Finally, you call! Of course he's here worrying himself sick. Why didn't you meet him at the station? He had to come here on foot. Okay, okay!... I'll let you speak to him. (*She hands the receiver to Ishmael.*)

ISHMAEL: Max, Max... (*He stares at the receiver, dumbfounded.*)

EMMA: What is it? What did he say?

ISHMAEL: He hung up!

EMMA: He hung up without saying anything?

ISHMAEL: He called me a bastard!

EMMA: I knew there was something fishy about you. Come on, tell me, what have you done?

ISHMAEL: I haven't done anything. Yes, I know, it doesn't look good. But I'm innocent.

EMMA: That's what all guilty people say. Okay. I'll let you go back to sleep. Then tomorrow, at the crack of dawn, out you go. (*She gets up and puts on a record. It's an aria sung by Jessye Norman and she listens reverently.*)

ISHMAEL: (*approaching her*) You're not so heartless as to throw me out like a dog when it's my first time in this town...

EMMA: You've never been to Paris before?

ISHMAEL: No, I went to medical school in Mexico. I know several Latin American countries, I know the United States and Canada. But I've never been to France, or Europe!

EMMA: Really! (*She sits down. He sits down next to her on the sofa-bed.*)

ISHMAEL: You're not really going to kick me out, are you? You're too kind. You wouldn't!

EMMA: Kind? Am I kind? I used to be. But after suffering so many blows, your heart hardens. From being unused, it dries up! At this point, I don't know if I'm kind...

ISHMAEL: (*his head on her knees*) Of course you're kind!

EMMA: (*caressing his face distractedly*) You hear that music? It's divine, isn't it? I adore it. It's my drug. When I feel horribly lonely, all it takes is a little shot of Jessye Norman or Barbara Hendricks and I feel fine again. I feel like I'm floating on a cloud. All my sorrows disappear. The new ones and the very old ones...

ISHMAEL: I knew you were kind. Kiss me!

SECOND TABLEAU

SCENE 1

The same set. Ishmael is alone. He is writing furiously. Then he raises his head.

ISHMAEL: He could have given me a chance to explain. He could have agreed to meet me, to listen to me. But no! Oh, I know them all too well with their uncompromising attitude. Uncompromising and ruthless! Anyway, I was doomed from the start. I'm paying. (*He gets up and paces back and forth.*) I'm paying for my father. And I'm paying for my mother. It's so unfair! Is it my fault he was a minister for two terms? Is it my fault she dragged me to every single birthday party at the presidential palace? Is it my fault I wasn't born in the slums of Bel Air? That I don't have an umbilical hernia and bandy legs? Everything would have been completely different. No one would have questioned anything I said.... No one would have scrutinized my actions. Being born on the right side of the tracks, that's the trick. (*He sits down again and starts writing. The door opens and Emma comes in. She's come from town and is dressed up.*) Finally! You certainly took your time!

EMMA: It's really cold outside. The last time we had weather like this was in 1952. I remember it because ...

ISHMAEL: So, how did you make out?

EMMA: Yes, it was in 1952. We set up on the stairs of the metro and fed soup to the poor.

ISHMAEL: Emma! How did you make out?

EMMA: I told you not to be so familiar with me!

ISHMAEL: Are you crazy or something?

EMMA: I don't like all these familiarities. Are you forgetting that

I'm not your age!

ISHMAEL: After what happened last night!

EMMA: You don't get it, do you? I did that to console you because you were so sad...but I don't love you. I already told you!

ISHMAEL: You don't really expect me to believe you've only done it with men you loved?

EMMA: Well, yes, actually! I see you coming a mile away. You think, here's a woman who was a nude dancer, so she's a whore. She made love to me because she's a whore. But that's not it at all. I pitied you and now I regret it.

ISHMAEL: What's gotten into you?

EMMA: I want to know why you left your country.

ISHMAEL: But I already told you. I needed a change! The air at home's unhealthy! (*Emma bursts out laughing, then she becomes serious. Ishmael approaches her to put his arm around her. She pushes him away.*) What's up, sweetheart?

EMMA: I told you, no familiarities!

ISHMAEL: You're really priceless! You make love to a guy. You whisper all kinds of sweet nothings in his ear. You even call him "my dearest, dearest, darling lover," and then you reject him!

EMMA: Tell me what happened!

ISHMAEL: Oh no, don't take that judgmental tone. I've had my fill of judges! Too many people telling me how to act. A revolutionary should do this. A militant should do that. I've had it up to here with banishment.

EMMA: Why weren't you waiting on the beach?

ISHMAEL: What?

EMMA: You were supposed to be on the beach at Labadie waiting for them with a group of supporters. Instead, when they got
there they found a detachment of soldiers and Tontons Macoutes.
Those who survived the slaughter were taken to Port-au-Prince
and no one knows what happened to them!

ISHMAEL: You've seen Max? You got this from him. Let's go find
him!

EMMA: He doesn't want to see you. He's too afraid of putting a
bullet in your head and landing behind bars. That's the way it
is in civilized countries. People are not supposed to take justice into their own hands. So bastards end up dying in bed!

ISHMAEL: Emma, you must believe me! I'm not the one who
sold them out to the police...

EMMA: Who was it then?

ISHMAEL: That's just what I keep wondering about! I was really
a much bigger fool and much more naive than I realized. And
right from the beginning, they had their eyes on me.

EMMA: You have about thirty deaths on your conscience.

ISHMAEL: I tell you, I'm not the guilty party.

EMMA: Okay, but you can't stay here!

ISHMAEL: Where do you want me to go? I have no papers. I don't
have a cent.

EMMA: Go on! Don't you think I know you have a numbered
Swiss account? That's how men like you operate!

ISHMAEL: A numbered Swiss account! Listen to me. Give me a
chance to explain. (*Pause.*) I didn't go back because I believed

in the regime, but because I couldn't bear living abroad any longer.

EMMA: There I can understand how you felt.

ISHMAEL: Do you know what it's like to see the sun shine over Hospital Hill?

EMMA: You have a Hospital Hill, too? Believe it or not, I grew up not far from there. There was this freight train loaded with sugar cane that used to roll slowly down the tracks. We children used to run after it and hang off the cars! Most of the girls weren't strong enough, but I was.

ISHMAEL: You know what it's like to walk in a crowd where everyone has the same color face as you? All of us black and together under the sun?

EMMA: Everyone's dark where you come from? Where I'm from, we have every color in the rainbow. Mama was yellow, high yellow, a chabine like we say. And Papa, he was real black, and he held himself very straight and proud under a crown of white hair.

ISHMAEL: I was fed up living far away, and speaking English and Spanish. I wanted to speak Creole, damn it! So I went back. And because of who I am—the son of one of the right-hand men in the old power structure—I was offered jobs. That was humiliating. It proved that no one believed in my student activism, my critical statements to the press, my repudiations. That regardless of what I did or said I remained a member of the privileged circle. No one took me seriously, I was a buffoon! (*Pause.*) I swear to you, it's not my fault the landing maneuver went wrong. It was badly planned. The work of amateurs. Like everything else. We counted on the cooperation of the peasants, but the peasants didn't help us. They let us be slaughtered down to the last man. Because the peasants don't give a damn if we want to play cowboys and Indians. They know that no matter what, they'll always get screwed. Screwed! (*He cries.*)

EMMA: Okay, don't get so riled up!

ISHMAEL: You're right. I'll go!

EMMA: Where? You don't know anyone in this city. (*Pause.*) I've always dreamed of having a man who would be all mine. Someone I wouldn't see only between four and five thirty because he had to get home to eat dinner with his wife, and because earlier he'd had a business lunch where he overate and overdrank. So, instead of making love, I'd have to run to the drugstore for baking soda! I'd like a man I could give pocket change to for his cigarettes and newspaper so long as he wouldn't read it while I sit in a corner, bored. You see, what I really need is a little tenderness. Can you give me that?

ISHMAEL: When a woman speaks of tenderness, she's talking slavery.

EMMA: Not always! All I'm asking for is your hand on my shoulder after we've made love, and your breath on my neck.

ISHMAEL: Is that all?

EMMA: Your eyes looking into mine, sometimes your smile. And understanding. Can you give me that?

ISHMAEL: I'll try ...

Blackout.

SCENE 2

The same set. Emma and Ishmael are seated opposite each other; on the table there are the remains of a meal. Ishmael is absorbed in the newspaper. He never glances at Emma who is looking at him adoringly.

ISHMAEL: What a bunch of asses! They don't understand anything about what's going on in Haiti. Look at what they've written.

EMMA: You cried out in your sleep again last night. Same old nightmare.

ISHMAEL: What a load of baloney! As far as I'm concerned, the son's worse than the father. Granted the father caused enormous bloodshed. Whole families were wiped out because one member was a suspected enemy. There was terror in the streets. But the son, that facade of so-called liberalism...

EMMA: And then you didn't want me!

ISHMAEL: (*finally looking at her*) Woman, no man is a machine. I'm not what you need! You need an obliging gigolo. I bet you've paid for two or three in your time. You've got enough money for that. Tell me, where does your money come from? A retired nude dancer, you should be starving to death. But no, you order meals from fancy caterers...

EMMA: I do it for you! I'd be happy with rice and codfish. That's what I like.

ISHMAEL: You've got champagne flowing like water.

EMMA: For you!

ISHMAEL: Answer my question. Where do you get all your money?

Emma gets up and struts up and down.

EMMA: There was a man who really loved me. An Argentinean. He was very rich.

ISHMAEL: Tell that to someone else!

EMMA: I swear it's the truth! His wife had just left him. He was very bitter. He gave me everything he owned.

ISHMAEL: *Tim tim bois sèche!*

EMMA: What?

ISHMAEL: Like the beginning of one of our fairy tales. You forgot to preface your story with it.

The doorbell rings. Ishmael jumps.

EMMA: It's Madame Renoux with the mail. You should know she comes at this time. (*She disappears into the hall. We hear her talk briefly. Ishmael gets up. As soon as Emma reappears, he throws himself on her.*) What's all this? Are you expecting a letter? (*He grabs the mail from her hands and examines it. Disappointed, he throws the letters on the floor. Then Emma pulls a letter from her bosom.*) Is this what you're expecting?

ISHMAEL: Give it to me.

She refuses. They fight. He gets the upper hand.

EMMA: Who is this letter from? Who is writing you here? Whom did you give this address to?

Ishmael reads, then collapses.

ISHMAEL: They've arrested her. That's it. They've arrested her.

EMMA: Who? Your wife? I'm surprised they'd arrest a foreigner. The worse they could do is deport her.

ISHMAEL: This is not about my wife.

EMMA: Who is it about then?

ISHMAEL: (*screaming*) She has nothing to do with all this. Nothing! She's innocent.

EMMA: Could you begin at the beginning?

ISHMAEL: What do you call the beginning? Was it being born into this god-forsaken family? The oldest son of a murderer?

EMMA: (*very gently*) Calm down, okay!

ISHMAEL: Isn't that my great misfortune? No one ever trusted me. No one ever took me seriously. Except her!

EMMA: Who are you talking about?

> *Ishmael calms himself and sits down. Then he lights a cigarette.*

ISHMAEL: I never loved my wife, I've told you that. But since I didn't want to take any more money from my parents and I didn't want to have anything—absolutely anything—more to do with them—you believe me, don't you?—I was penniless. She fed me, took me in, took care of me. Thanks to her, I finished medical school. We got married. We had two children. Two sons. It wasn't bliss, but life was okay. And then one day, I told you, I went home. She came too. My parents were deliriously happy. You can imagine, the prodigal son returning to the fold. Let's kill the fatted calf. They offered us a villa in Kenscoff.

EMMA: The good life, huh?

ISHMAEL: Maybe! But I didn't want any part of that life! I was disgusted with myself, you understand! They offered me everything, even the position of Minister of Health. I turned it down. *Turned it down.* I preferred to work in my clinic.

EMMA: I imagine you made money just the same.

ISHMAEL: Yes, but it was clean money! And then one day, I needed a nurse and she showed up...

EMMA: Who, she?

ISHMAEL: Clorinda.

EMMA: Clorinda! You Haitians have some names!

ISHMAEL: Yes, Clorinda! And she breathed fresh air into my life. Beckoning like a glass of pure spring water. She was beautiful. Her skin was black with almost a bluish tint, her eyes sparkled in the darkness of her face, and her mouth when she laughed was round and purplish like a plum.

EMMA: (*jealous*) My God!

ISHMAEL: Beautiful, you hear! And it's for her sake that I wanted to become a man. I wanted to deserve her admiration, her respect. So I got mixed up with the group that wanted to overthrow Jean-Claude. I offered them my contacts, everything I knew. They weren't interested at first. They didn't trust me. Same old story. "But isn't he Modestin's son?" And then, little by little, they accepted me...

EMMA: To their misfortune!

ISHMAEL: But she didn't know anything about any of this. She didn't believe in politics, she saw it as a dirty, dangerous game. Why did they arrest her? (*Pause.*) Emma, what can I do? You know what jails are like in Haiti?

EMMA: Like everywhere, I guess. Jail is jail. It's never much fun!

ISHMAEL: I can't keep going around in circles. You have to arrange for me to see Max.

EMMA: He doesn't want to see you.

ISHMAEL: He must. You don't condemn a man without hearing him out. I'm not the one who sold them out to the Tontons Macoutes! I don't know where the leak came from. Didn't the Popular Union boast from Venezuela that they were preparing a landing? Didn't Joseph Mondésir make some wild announcements on American TV? They were on their guard, that's all. I have no reason to reproach myself.

EMMA: Nevertheless!

ISHMAEL: What do you think I should have done?

EMMA: When you found out from your mother that they'd gotten wind of your plans, because she warned you several days before...

ISHMAEL: The night before. She told me the night before. There wasn't anything I could do to stop the operation at that point. Obviously you think I should have stayed and played the hero, gone down with a bullet in my head or rotted in prison? I thought that no matter what, I had to find my friends so we could learn from this failure. That's why I left.

EMMA: You were afraid, that's all there is to it.

ISHMAEL: Okay, I was afraid. But above all I wanted to find answers, I wanted to understand why our history is such a record of mistakes, aborted plans, failed landings. What is it that is dead in us? From Africa to the Americas, we are on our knees...

EMMA: You're wrong. Things are moving in South Africa. Haven't you been watching television? Things are moving in your country, too. In my opinion, Jean-Claude won't last much longer.... When I see those demonstrations, those raised fists, I'm reminded of my youth.

ISHMAEL: Your youth?

EMMA: What's so funny? I might have been a nude dancer but that doesn't mean I don't have a militant past! You know, the revolution doesn't only attract sons of bourgeois like you! It attracts everyone. Paralytics in wheelchairs, invalids in hospital beds. Whores and homosexuals...

ISHMAEL: What am I going to do? I must call Max!

He rushes to the phone. Emma takes the receiver from his hands.

EMMA: But he doesn't want to talk to you! Can't you get that through your thick skull?

ISHMAEL: She's innocent. When I used to spin my dreams in front of her, she would shrug her shoulders and say: "There's no happiness for the black man!" You see, her two brothers were stuck in a prison camp in Miami. One of her sisters was a prostitute in the Dominican Republic. She had her doubts about me, and I was dying to brighten her eyes with hope. What am I going to do?

EMMA: You can't do anything. She might be dead by now!

ISHMAEL: Dead! You're heartless , rejoicing in my misfortune!

EMMA: No, I'm not rejoicing. If you really want to know, I don't give a damn about you or your Clorinda. Clorinda! (*She goes over to the stereo to put on a record.*)

ISHMAEL: (*jumping up*) Oh no, not another one of your damned arias! I can't figure out how a black woman can like that kind of music!

EMMA: The singers are black !

ISHMAEL: Then you're all a bunch of lunatics!

EMMA: How can you be so limited? So for you, the only real music is ka.... When I was at the New Venus a musician who loved me very much wrote a song for me. (*She starts to hum and strut up and down as is her habit.*)

ISHMAEL: Do you know the merengue from back home?

EMMA: Someone gave me an album of Haitian music! (*She looks for it and finds it.*) See, here it is!

ISHMAEL: (*grabs it out of her hands*) Let me see it. It's not great, but it'll do! (*He puts the record on and starts dancing.*) Now that's what I call music! Let's dance! (*They dance. He kisses her.*) Not bad. Okay! I take back everything I just said. Maybe you like opera, but you are a real black woman.

EMMA: What's a real black woman?

ISHMAEL: Like you. One who knows how to dance. (*They laugh.*) Oh la! One Saturday night, I'd like to take you to a place called the Lambi. It used to really shock people that I, a doctor, would spend time in a place like that. I would hold Clorinda tight and... (*He lets go of Emma.*) Clorinda! My God, what am I going to do? (*Suddenly the doorbell rings.*) What's that?

EMMA: (*just as scared*) The mail has already been delivered!

ISHMAEL: Go see, damn it! Let's get it over with!

> *Emma obeys. We can hear her speaking to someone in the hall. She reenters.*

EMMA: It was Madame Renoux again. It seems some men came by to question her.

ISHMAEL: To question her?

EMMA: They wanted to know if she had seen anyone suspicious around here.

ISHMAEL: Suspicious? So it was the police?

EMMA: She doesn't know. They weren't wearing uniforms.

ISHMAEL: Just like that, strangers show up at her place, quiz her, and she answers!

EMMA: Don't worry. Madame Renoux is okay!

ISHMAEL: What happened? Tell me...

EMMA: The men asked if there were any new tenants or new faces around! But maybe it's nothing to worry about. We're so close to Barbès with all those illegal Arabs and Africans, it's not surprising they check things out periodically. No one is going to come and take you away from me, don't be afraid .

ISHMAEL: I've got to leave. I've got to leave right away.

EMMA: Where do you want to go? This is the safest place for you to be.

ISHMAEL: The coward! The bastard! He put the police on my tail. Oh they're real noble, these revolutionaries...

EMMA: Who are you talking about?

ISHMAEL: About Max of course! Who else knows I'm hiding here?

EMMA: He wouldn't do that!

ISHMAEL: You don't know these people. They have no pity. Whoever's not with them is against them, and then it's lights out, no pity. When I lived in Mexico City, it was always like that: gangland killings. One faction blowing the lid on another. That's why we never get anywhere. We're not united.

EMMA: Calm down. You're not in Mexico City anymore. You're in Paris with me, Emma. I've told you before, and I'll tell you again, as long as you're with me, nothing can happen to you.

Do you believe me?

Ishmael remains silent.

EMMA: You don't know how many men I've held against me and
cured of their fears. They would come to me all knotted up, bitter, frustrated. And all it took was a few words, a few gestures.
Come on. Come here, closer. Stretch out. Close your eyes. Sh!
There, don't you feel better?

THIRD TABLEAU

The room is silent and dark. Ishmael is still sleeping. Emma sits at the foot of his bed.

EMMA: How easily he sleeps! When I was little, I always had trouble going to sleep. Mama would sing me songs by Tino Rossi. (*She laughs, then sings.*) "Stay in my arms Marinella , I want to stay with you until the morning light," (*she gets up and does several dance steps*) "dancing this rumba of love." (*She laughs.*) Or else: (*singing again*) "As long as there'll be stars under the vault of heaven, beggars will find joy in the brightness of night..." Mama had a beautiful voice. Not like me. I used to stay curled up against her, enveloped in the fragrance of her perfume. Papa didn't approve. He would scream: "Julienne, stop that foolishness and leave that child alone!" I wonder if he wasn't jealous! Of course, he must have been! When she heard his voice, Mama would blow out the lamp— we didn't have electricity—and she would leave me alone in the dark. In the dark and scared. (*Pause.*) Now, she's the one who's alone in the dark. *An ba là tè, pa ni chouval bwa*, there's no merry-go-round underground. I only hope she's not afraid. (*Pause.*) Sometimes, I tell myself that they lied. That she's still there. That if I took the boat.... The boat? What am I saying? There are no more boats. People fly nowadays. How long does it take to get to Pointe-à-Pitre from Paris? Four or five hours? It's not good for the blood, these sudden changes. Cold today, a scorcher tomorrow.... Yes, sometimes, I tell myself that they tricked me and she'll be there waiting for me at Raizet airport. Short and small under her white hair. In the black dress she always wore after the death of my brother Jose. A drunk and an idler, that's what my brother was. He killed himself coming back from a wedding where he had had too much to drink. But as soon as he was dead, everyone started to mourn for him as if he'd been a saint. Mama kept a candle lit in front of his picture. All you have to do is die. So maybe when I die, they'll stop whispering, "stripper, nude dancer" and start talking about my qualities. (*Pause.*) Yes, Mama'll be there waiting for me and I'll crawl back into her womb. Once inside, nothing and no one will ever make me be born again. I've had it with life! Had it! When I was little... but why do I keep talking about my childhood? It's ridiculous! Worse than ridiculous, unhealthy.... It's just that I didn't see time creeping up on me. It played a dirty trick on me. One day, I looked at myself in the mirror and I was old. Old and ugly. Wrinkles around the mouth. Rings under the eyes. Bags. That's what an English lover once used to say to me. (*Imitating an English accent*) "My dear, you have bags under the eyes." (*She laughs.*) Not very kind, that man. Always making fun of me. It seems that's English humor. (*She laughs.*) Luckily, I didn't get fat. My body is still slim. (*She gets up and struts about. At this point, Ishmael grunts and moans in his sleep. She goes over to him.*) It's okay. I'm right here. Nothing will happen to you. They won't get you even if you are what they say: a traitor and a sell-out. How I wish I were like him! A man. Handsome. A doctor. A father who's a Minister. He has everything going for him and still he isn't happy. Mama used to say: "Happiness is like the feathery flower of the silk-cotton tree. Everyone chases after it, but no one can catch it... Mama, I'm afraid. (*Pause.*) And of what, good God? Emma, stop, this is no time to act like a fool. For once that you've found a man to keep you warm.

FOURTH TABLEAU

SCENE 1

The room is in a terrible mess. Ishmael enters, coming from the other room. He is distraught and feverish.

ISHMAEL: The money's got to be here. She must hide it somewhere, the old bag, the old cow! Because she's rolling in it. (*Imitating her*) "Mr. Etiennne, I'd like a leg of lamb. Madame Jeannette, put aside a striped bass for me. Nicholas, do you have any Saumur wine?" I'd like to see the bills she must have. But she's cunning. She never pays for anything in front of me. She goes out and disappears for hours on end, while I... (*He starts searching again.*) She's the kind of woman who doesn't believe in banks. The kind that likes to have her nest egg close at hand. Still, I've looked everywhere. Under the mattresses, under the linen, in the dressers, in the closets. Even in all those photo albums she keeps in her drawers. It would be easy to slide a wad of bills between the pages. Nothing. Nothing but dust and roaches. Maybe she has a checkbook in her handbag. That would be easiest of all because it's a cinch to imitate her signature. Emma in a grand flourish. Regal as if the old whore took herself for someone high class! Boisgris in tiny letters. How does it work here? If I forged her signature at the bottom of the check, would they give me the money? Or would they ask me for an ID? God! (*He collapses, then gets up again.*) I've got to find some money. I've got to get away. Like my mother used to say, money rules the world. As soon as I get my hands on some cash, I can find someone to sell me a passport. There must be forgers around! Poor Ishmael, you think you're in the middle of a detective novel! Trench coat collar turned up, dark glasses. (*He laughs, then collapses again. He gets up momentarily.*) The bathroom, I haven't looked in the bathroom yet. In the box of old newspapers! (*He runs out of the room. After a moment, Emma enters, coming from outside. She too seems feverish, and at first she doesn't notice the disarray.*)

EMMA: Ishmael, Ishmael! (*Pause.*) My God, where is he? Ishmael!

As she begins to panic, he reappears.

ISHMAEL: Back so soon?

EMMA: You gave me a terrible fright! I'm always afraid when I leave you ...

ISHMAEL: Of what?

EMMA: I've been afraid ever since the police came to question Madame Renoux. You know, the imagination runs wild. I start to think Max and his goons could come and settle accounts..

ISHMAEL: Accounts? Kill me, that's what you mean! Unlikely! They're too cowardly for that. I'd actually prefer it: a kind of People's Court. "Comrade Ishmael Modestin, you have betrayed the revolution. We condemn you to death. Bang, bang, bang. Three bullets in the head." No, they'll let me die a slow death!

EMMA: Who's talking about dying! I won't let you die. You must live. You know why I came back so quickly? (*At this point, she notices the disorder in the room.*) Who opened all the drawers? Who knocked over the lamp? Who... (*She turns completely around, then faces Ishmael again.*) Did you do all this? But... but.... What were you...?

ISHMAEL: Emma, I must leave.

EMMA: Money, you were looking for money!

ISHMAEL: Try to understand, I've got to get out of here!

EMMA: You wanted to rob me!

ISHMAEL: Emma!

EMMA: I've been such a stupid fool! Giving him pink grapefruit for his breakfast in the morning. Columbian coffee. A cup of verbena tea at night. And he tries to rob me! I go out to look for a nice filet and during that time, he tries to rob me!

ISHMAEL: Don't you realize I don't give a damn about your filets, your Saumur wine, your pink grapefruits? I really don't give a shit. Oh, you've learned your lesson well. To keep your man happy, stuff his belly. Make him some tasty little dishes. My wife was the same! And she didn't realize that her tasty little dishes made me sick! The same goes for you. You make me sick! You hear me? I can do without your flabby breasts, the wrinkled skin on your neck, your jello-like stomach and your pussy. Especially your insatiable pussy. A big, slobbering mouth that wants to swallow me whole.

EMMA: Shut up, Ishmael!

ISHMAEL: No, I won't shut up. Because I can't anymore! Week after week I've had to put up with your stories about nude dancing, and Marie-Galante, and your mother whose grave you never saw. You know you've got a screw loose, Emma? You should be locked up in an asylum.

EMMA: So, you lied when you said you loved me.

ISHMAEL: When did I ever say that? You nagged the hell out of me: "Darling, dearest darling, do you love me? Tell me, will you stay with me forever?" So I said yes just so I'd have some peace. Do you remember there were some nights when I'd shut myself up in the bathroom for so long that you'd start banging on the door? That was so I wouldn't have to listen to you. You know, before meeting you, I never made love on command.

> *She throws herself on him in order to hit him. They struggle fiercely for a few minutes. She falls down with a scream then stays on the floor, motionless.*

ISHMAEL: Get up, I tell you. (*He bends over her.*)

EMMA: Is what you just said true?

ISHMAEL: Of course not!

EMMA: I make you sick?

ISHMAEL: *No, no*! But she's on my mind all the time. I've got to leave. I have to get back to Haiti!

EMMA: You're crazy!

ISHMAEL: You see, I'm a pretty rotten guy. When you come down to it, I've betrayed everyone. My family and my class, those who wanted me to take a seat at the grand banquet of the exploiters. The comrades who died on the beach at Labadie. My wife. My children. But her, I don't want to betray...

EMMA: You love her that much?

ISHMAEL: Yes. (*Silence. Emma is visibly hurt.*) You asked, that's the truth. I can't stand the thought that something might happen to her because of me. I have to go back to clear her.

EMMA: They'll kill you!

ISHMAEL: Not me! Are you forgetting who I am? My father will call Jean-Claude.... They'll lecture me, I'll hang down my head, and then I'll go back to my clinic, my patients, my villa in Kenscoff, my wife, my sons ...

EMMA: (*cruelly*) They've probably already killed her by now!

ISHMAEL: No. Something tells me she's still alive.

EMMA: What about me? Have you given me any thought?

ISHMAEL: You?

EMMA: (*after a pause*) Yes, me... I was fine—well almost fine—all alone with my memories, and then you came along and I started loving you...

ISHMAEL: Come with me, Emma ... (*His voice, restrained at first, gradually warms up.*) Yes, come with me. Guadeloupe, Haiti, isn't it all the same? Aren't we the same people come out of the same bellies of the same slave ships? (*Emma gets up.*) Don't we speak a similar Creole? And aren't our proverbs and tales the same ? For hyena, you say *zamba*, and I say *bouki*, but we're talking about the same animal.

EMMA: We'll live near Hospital Hill. A house with a courtyard, and a garden filled with tamarind and coolie plum trees. I'll make jam. In good weather, we'll see Marie-Galante... I'll go sit in the cemetery and say to Mama... "Mama, your child has come home. Tired and weary. My feet are bleeding from walking through life without shoes..."

ISHMAEL: (*holding and rocking her like a child*) Come, come!

EMMA: I'll tell her: "I never stopped loving and respecting you even when I disrespected myself." Do you think she'll understand and forgive me?

ISHMAEL: There's nothing to forgive you for, Emma. You're as pure as a newborn child. (*Pause.*) They were wrong to think I was a coward. I simply needed someone weaker than me to protect!

> *Emma gets up. All the tenderness and emotion that had developed between her and Ishmael vanish.*

EMMA: Me, weak! If I were weak, I'd be dead!

ISHMAEL: But of course you're weak. Let me play my role.

EMMA: Meaning what?

ISHMAEL: I've always dreamed of a woman who'd be like a small child in my life, and in my arms. I'll feed her, teach her to talk. I'll whisper to her what she should say. The only voice she'd obey would be mine. Devotion! Can you give me that?

EMMA: I never know where you're coming from! When I try to be nice, you snap at me!

ISHMAEL: That's not it! What you want is to tie me up, enslave me, destroy me with your kindness. Make me into a spineless man, limp all over except for my penis! Same as my wife! All that sweetness and submission were nothing but a trap... Clorinda's the only one who was different. For her, I was handsome...

EMMA: It's true, you're not bad-looking!

ISHMAEL: I was smart!

EMMA: That's true too!

ISHMAEL: She admired me, you understand. In her eyes, I saw myself as noble, generous, courageous. In your eyes, I'm small, very small, ridiculously small.

EMMA: (*after a pause*) Were you serious a few minutes ago? (*Ishmael doesn't respond.*) When you talked about taking me with you?

ISHMAEL: Of course I was! Haiti, Martinique, Guadeloupe, Barbados and Jamaica, aren't they all the same? Sugar cane, thousands of exiles, the heavy hand of oppression!

EMMA: When I take my nap in the middle of the afternoon, I'll sweat so much my underclothes will stick to me.... How much does it cost to fly to Haiti?

ISHMAEL: I've forgotten... Enough daydreams, anyhow. You forget I don't have papers. The permit my friends forged for me has expired.

EMMA: Don't worry about that.... Tell me what life will be like over there?

Ishmael hesitates, then plays along.

ISHMAEL: It will be a like a cup of hot chocolate! You know when I was little, there was a woman who used to work for us. Her name was Sandrine!

EMMA: Sandrine! What a pretty name! Mama's name was Julienne!

ISHMAEL: Every morning before I would leave for school, she made me drink a cup of hot chocolate. She put lemon peel in it, a pinch of cinnamon, and I drank it boiling hot, but it was so sweet to my stomach.... That's what our life will taste like!

EMMA: Ishmael, my love, my very own man, hold me tighter than tight!

SCENE 2

The same set. Emma is dressed as if she had just come in from outside. Ishmael is as exuberant as a child and is examining a passport.

ISHMAEL: Ishmael Modestin born in Jacmel, that's me. Me. And this is an EEC passport, from the European Economic Community. I'm a European now. Don't I look like one? Thank you, Mama! (*He goes to hug her. She pushes him away, coldly.*)

EMMA: I've already told you not to call me Mama.

ISHMAEL: But, my love, you are my mother! More so than the high-class harlot who gave birth to me. You're my mother, my sister, my lover, my everything.... But how did you get this passport?

EMMA: Through a man who once loved me very much. He was high up in the police department. And he kept his connections.

ISHMAEL: A cop, in other words! Well, you certainly hung out with the right people! Let me see the airplane tickets.... Paris/ New York/ Port-au-Prince. Didn't I tell you to get an Air France flight with a stopover in Guadeloupe?

EMMA: Air France was full. It's Christmas time. Lots of people are going home to spend the holidays with their families. A little parenthesis of happiness and warmth dropped into the greyness of the year.

ISHMAEL: I think it's mostly tourists who pack the airplanes.

EMMA: Not at all. It seems this is a very bad year for tourism. With all the separatists' bombs. The last one killed an American. Poor devil! You go on vacation and end up dead.

ISHMAEL: You're not going to start crying over some American. Are you crazy or what?

EMMA: You know I'm crazy. That's what you spend your time telling me.... Ishmael, do you believe in the independence of Guadeloupe? It's strange, when I was little, everyone saw themselves as French, more French than the French! One of Mama's sisters was born on July 14th, Bastille Day, the national holiday. Her family was so proud, you'd think her mother had deliberately planned it!

ISHMAEL: Let me have the travelers cheques!

EMMA: I got dollars instead.

ISHMAEL: Dollars! But what if we lose them! What if they're stolen! It's obvious you never travel! (*He counts them, and stops.*) Five hundred! That's all you got? How long will that last? Boy, are you miserly!

EMMA: With the rate of the dollar, that's not so bad, you know. Six and a half francs to the dollar!

ISHMAEL: Used to be ten francs. I'd like to have seen you then. I hate having to go through New York! There's always some lousy Haitian hanging around the airport and the next day you see your photo on the front page of the *Haitian Observer*! I can imagine what people will say when they find out I've gone back home. They won't understand a thing and once again they'll make up a story. "After betraying his comrades, Ishmael Modestin comes home to claim his reward...." What do you think of the pompous style of our journalists? All they talk about are traitors and puppets...

EMMA: Ishmael, did you notice anything? (*Pause.*) Did you notice that I only got one airplane ticket?

ISHMAEL: Only one? No! Why? I thought you were keeping yours with your things. Only one...

EMMA: How would I have fit in in Haiti? What did you have in store for me?

ISHMAEL: In store for you?

EMMA: Yes.

ISHMAEL: Well, you're a very resourceful woman. You know what
I see you doing? Running a hotel...

EMMA: You mean a brothel!

ISHMAEL: This is no time to be making jokes. A hotel! Not a big
concern like Oloffson's or the Ibo Lele. No, a small, more inti-
mate kind of place where the owner's personality is important.
A family hotel. I even came up with a name: "The Tropical Breeze"...

EMMA: "The Tropical Breeze Hotel?" (*She bursts out laughing.*)
How corny can you get! You might be a good doctor, but you
have zero imagination. "The Tropical Breeze Hotel." It's like
the people who wanted to christen me "Silver Moon!" (*She laughs,
then stares at him.*) You never believed I'd come with you, did
you? (*Pause.*) What were you going to do if I had? Ditch me at
the airport? Abandon me like those French people who leave
their dogs and cats by the side of the highway when they go on
vacation? Or, before leaving, were you going to knock me over
the head with a bottle so I wouldn't run after you?

ISHMAEL: Come with me, Emma.

EMMA: You know, I would have loved to come back with a man
at my side. Where I come from, that's the only way a woman can
get any respect. By having a man at her side! And what a man!
A doctor!... But that will never be; we won't ever have a house
with a courtyard, and a garden full of bougainvillea and hibis-
cus. And there won't be any tamarind or coolie plum trees.

ISHMAEL: I can see them waiting for me at the airport! "There's
that son of a bitch, Modestin's son. What kind of bullshit does
he have up his sleeve this time?" My father and mother are there.
And my wife and my two sons! Emma, don't let me go alone!

EMMA: I would have loved to grow roses. Not Cayenne roses, but French roses. Mama loved roses. They wrote me that her casket was covered with them. White, mauve, crimson...! I'd have loved to have a child with you! A girl. She would have had Mama's smile and her eyes. People would say, "She looks like her grandmother, but darker." That's what they said about me. "She looks just like her mother, but darker." What a shame, Ishmael, that we met each other so late! Things might have been different. We might have sat side by side in the lecture hall. We might have studied for our exams together. We might both have become doctors. You a cardiologist and me a gynecologist! Life's just not fair!

ISHMAEL: Emma, they're going to kill me!

EMMA: No, they aren't! You said yourself they wouldn't do anything to you! Let me give you a bit of advice though: put your life in order. Get a divorce from your wife...

ISHMAEL: She would never give me one!

EMMA: Marry your Clorinda...

ISHMAEL: Emma!

EMMA: What? We could've named our little girl Alexandra. I've always loved that name. She wouldn't have been familiar with winter, freezing maid's rooms, racism, or fear. No one would have said to her, "Take off your blouse. Cross your legs. Higher. Turn around." She wouldn't know exile. She wouldn't shed blood on life's mean streets!

ISHMAEL: Emma!

EMMA: I packed a suitcase for you. Here it is! How would I have fit in with your bourgeois tribunal?

ISHMAEL: Listen, if you don't like my idea of a family hotel, you could open a dance school. Like Katherine Dunham! I bet you students would flock to it from all over the world.

EMMA: Nude dancers don't have to know how to dance. A beautiful ass is all it takes!

ISHMAEL: Or then you could run...

EMMA: A whorehouse, right? A whorehouse for Tontons Macoutes. "Gentlemen, please take off your dark glasses. In here, we make love not war." (*She laughs. He looks at her. She stops.*) Okay, okay. It's not funny!

ISHMAEL: A restaurant! You could open a restaurant. You're the best cook I know.

EMMA: That's not what you used to say. You were always criticizing me!

ISHMAEL: Emma, you're not going to end your life here. Can you imagine what it's like to be old in Paris?

EMMA: I'm already old!

ISHMAEL: You, old! Not at all! You're young, Emma, and you're beautiful too! Emma, just think of what it will be like. A complexion dulled by too many winters, eyes vacant from waiting in vain for a glimpse of the sun, and at the end, a pile of bones in the Montparnasse cemetery!

EMMA: That's where Sartre is buried. Not such bad company! You made me think of something! Up until a few months ago, I used to see an old black woman in the market. All stooped over, with her big shopping basket. Her grey hair all balled up like Mama's used to be. Practically blind.

ISHMAEL: I'll build a house for you in Bois Verna ...

EMMA: Too late. I don't see her any more. She must have died! (*Pause.*) Go on. Take your suitcase.

ISHMAEL: If you leave me, I'll start messing up all over again. I'll play the revolutionary, and chase after women. I'll start drinking again. Yes, drinking, and you don't like men who drink. You were always snatching the bottle of rum out of my hands.

EMMA: You better go now. I put a bottle of that aftershave you like in your suitcase.

FIFTH TABLEAU

The same room. It is night and the lamp is lit. Emma is wearing the same outfit as in the first scene, but it is dirty. She is untidy, and looks older. A record comes to an end. It's Haitian music, Toto Bissainthe for example. She gets up and puts the needle back to the beginning. For several minutes, she listens carefully.

EMMA: Their Creole is weird! Impossible to understand. (*She listens again, then moves away and sits on the sofa. She remains silent for a long time.*) Where is he now? Maybe his plane crashed. No! Don't the papers always claim that air travel is the safest form of travel? The roads in France are deadlier than all the Boeings put together... When I was young, we traveled by boat, not plane. We docked in Dieppe or Le Havre. From there, we took the boat train. The station in Paris was thick with black people. (*Laughter, followed by another long period of silence*) I came over on the Katoumba. One of those Greek liners. At the farewell ball, the captain said to me: "I would love to see you "shimmy". "Shimmy!" He thought he was talking Creole. I was annoyed at his familiarity and I gave him a dirty look. I never liked people taking liberties. At the New Venus, they used to say I was proud. (*She gets up and struts about. Then she sits down again.*) I would have loved to go home with him at my arm! Where I come from, that's the only way a woman can get any respect. She could catch the moon, bite into it and drag it home between her teeth, it's all for naught if she doesn't have a man. I've been courted by a lot of men. I can even honestly say that a lot of men have been crazy about me. But not one of them proposed to me. Mama used to say: "Marriage is like a Russian pantomime" (*She laughs.*) A Russian pantomime! Mama had some of the weirdest ideas! She's the one who would have been happy to see me come back home with a man. But unfortunately, she never will.... You'd think he might at least have sent me a card with a few words on it: "My dear Emma, thanks for everything." But no, he's back with his Clorinda, assuming they haven't killed her. (*She laughs maliciously.*) Oh, they have some names these Haitians. That's the way it was back home, too. People gave the most far-fetched names to their children. One of my friends at school was called Aude, after the pale, white maiden in the *Song of Roland*. When he stood up, a strapping black fellow, everyone shrieked with laughter. Parents are merciless.... (*Pause.*) Max was furious that I let him get away, that I actually helped him get away. He bawled me out on the phone. "He's a beast, a dangerous character. He's got thirty deaths on his conscience." Thirty deaths plus one. *One.* (*Pause.*) Anyhow, their Hospital Hill isn't the real Hospital Hill. There are no sugar cane freight trains with little black children hanging off the back. There are no tamarind trees and no coolie plum trees. There's only razor-sharp Guinea grass.... I should go see a doctor but I already know what he's going to say: "It's your age, Ma'am!" "Your age!" It's strange, I feel like I was born yesterday. Mama wanted a boy, and she was disappointed. As for Papa, he refused to lay eyes on me for three days! He was something, Papa. I wonder if he had a heart. "That child brings dishonor to our name." (*Pause.*) Every day I ask Madame Renoux, but there's nothing. Nothing. Just bills. Gas and electric and telephone. Maybe his plane was hijacked? With all the terrorists out there! That's all you see on television. Maybe he's dead? His burned body lying in the midst of the wreckage... but no, he's alive. He's alive and he's forgotten all about me. (*Mimicking a third person*) My dear Emma, you're making a big mistake getting all worked up over this young man. This young man with bad manners who doesn't bother to say thank you. (*She puts Toto Bissainthe's record back on and sits down.*) What is she saying? (*The telephone rings.*) Who could that be, at this hour? (*The telephone keeps ringing. She hesitates a moment, then rushes awkwardly to answer it.*) Coming, coming. (*She picks up the phone.*) Hello, hello! Oh, it's you Max! What do you want now?... Whether I've been watching TV? Listening to the news?... Jean-Claude Duvalier has been unseated? What does that mean? Overthrown? Oh, overthrown? Well, that's good!... Some people have been arrested? You hope they'll be executed?... Oh, no, no! He wasn't involved in any of that! Oh, no, he wasn't an agent. He went back to save Clorinda. Max, are you sure he's been arrested? But he's innocent! Max! (*Max has hung up. She stands there staring at the phone, then she puts it down gently.*) So that's it. What terrible luck. (*She sits down.*) After all, what does all this have to do with me? Why am I so worried? (*She returns to the mirror and starts making herself up. Slowly at first, then faster and faster, trans-forming her face into a clown's face.*) None of this is any of my business! Just a little bit more! Fine, that's it. I'll stick on my false eyelashes and the show can begin!

≈

DENISE BONAL

BEWARE THE HEART

Translated from the French by

RICHARD MILLER

UBU REPERTORY THEATER PUBLICATIONS
NEW YORK

Denise Bonal was born in Algeria and began her long and varied theater career at the age of twelve, when her family moved to Paris. From 1951 to 1971 she performed and toured with regional theater companies, all the while perfecting her writing. Since 1971, she has led a career not only as an actress, but as a writer and teacher as well. *Légère en août* (1974) was performed in Paris, Athens and throughout Belgium. Her prize-winning *Les Moutons de la nuit* was presented in Paris in 1976. *Honorée par un petit monument* was one of six plays selected to represent contemporary theater in Quebec in 1978, and was later presented at the International Festival in Lyon and at the Avignon Festival. It was produced in Paris by the National Theater of Chaillot in 1980. *Lit vers Léthé*, written under the pseudonym Luis Aftel, was produced at the Chapelle de la Salpétrière in Paris in 1983. *Family Portrait*, first presented as a staged reading at Ubu Repertory Theater in 1985, was produced at the Théâtre de l'Est Parisien (TEP) in 1986 and at Ubu Repertory Theater in 1992. The following year, *A Picture Perfect Sky* (*Passions et prairie*) also published by Ubu, premiered at the TEP in Paris. Her two most recent plays are *Beware the Heart* (*Féroce comme le coeur*, 1992), broadcast on Radio France–Culture in 1994, and *Dérives et petits détails* (1993), which was given a public reading at Théâtre Ouvert in Paris in October, 1993. Bonal was awarded two prizes by the Société des Auteurs et Compositeurs Dramatiques, in 1980 and in 1986, and was named a fellow of the Centre National des Lettres in 1981. In 1988 she was awarded the Arletty Prize for best woman playwright in the French-language theater. She taught for a number of years at the French National School of Dramatic Arts in Paris. Denise Bonal was a member of the Board of Directors of the SACD from 1988 through 1991.

Richard Miller has translated many works of fiction and nonfiction, from Balzac to Barthes, as well as a number of plays for Ubu Repertory Theater. His translations of Paul Emond's *Talk About Love!* and Michèle Fabien's *Jocasta* were both staged at Ubu during the 1993 fall season. He is currently translating Jean-Marie Besset's new play, *Marie Hasparren*. He lives in Paris.

Beware the Heart, in Richard Miller's translation, had its first staged reading at Ubu Repertory Theater, 15 West 28th Street, New York, NY 10001, on April 18th, 1994.

CHARACTERS

FERNAND, *The Father*

CAMILLE, *The elder daughter*

CHLOE, *The younger daughter*

BENOITE , *The Mother*

RICHARD, *The Son*

JOSEPH, *The Visitor*

MRS. RONSARD, *The Neighbor*

ACT I

WHY HIM?

Richard, Camille, Chloe, sitting apart from each other in silence. Fernand enters wearing a hat, which he never removes.

FERNAND: So, what's going on? When I left, everything was fine, not a cloud in the sky. I come back, it's "man the lifeboats," a heavy fog has moved in. (*Pause.*) Has the cat died?

CAMILLE: She's going to have kittens.

FERNAND: Your mother's sick. And she won't admit it? (*The three children shake their heads "no."*) At night, when I'm on my way home from making my rounds, sometimes I see the cows standing at the side of the road, just staring up at the stars, waiting... And then I know I'll find everything in order here, everyone well... (*Pause.*)...And if the cows aren't there, then I know there's going to be something wrong.

CAMILLE: And were there cows at the side of the road tonight?

FERNAND: Not a single one.

CAMILLE: They know.

FERNAND: Tell me all about it. (*Everyone is silent.*) Where is Benoîte?

RICHARD: She's preparing.

FERNAND: For what?

RICHARD: To prepare us.

A pause. Benoîte enters, kisses Fernand and sits down. Her latent, pent-up energy is obvious. She takes a deep breath and does not speak until she feels ready.

171

BENOITE: We're going to discuss the whole thing together. In detail. Calmly. We won't be nervous and we won't be suspicious.

FERNAND: Is it going to be something serious?

BENOITE: How long did you say, Chloe? Two, three weeks?

CHLOE: More or less...

BENOITE: Yes, of course...how can anyone tell... Let's say a month and a half.

FERNAND: What's going on?

BENOITE: I told you all about it last night, Fernand...

FERNAND: You did?

BENOITE: I never want to have to say someday that I refused (*breaking off, in an aside to Fernand*)—and who was that man, then, with his cold feet, who was in my bed at three o'clock this morning, telling me about sugar bowls, I wonder?—(*returning to the subject*) that I refused to open our home to a person in the direst need. I'd never be able to forgive myself until the day I died, and dying without being able to do that is like dying twice. Once is enough.

> *Silence. No one dares ask a direct question. Fernand, after looking at all of them, ventures to ask one.*

FERNAND: And just who is it who's in the "direst need?"

BENOITE: We're all going to be called upon to show more than courage, more than patience.

RICHARD: When you say "more than," what exactly do you mean?

BENOITE: I mean that we'll have to keep smiling.

FERNAND: I'm trying to smile, but it doesn't seem to be working.

BENOITE: We're a family that keeps its word. If we decide to do something, we do it. We'll manage. I'm sure of it. (*Silence. As if in reply:*) I can't bear to look around at all the barbarism in the world, at all the people with their heads buried in the sand, like ostriches.

FERNAND: (*interrogatively, to the others*) I guess I'm missing something.

CAMILLE: Where's he going to sleep?

BENOITE: In our room.

FERNAND: (*to the children*) Did you hear what I heard?

CAMILLE: And where will you sleep?

BENOITE: In the room at the back.

Fernand rises to speak. Richard cuts in.

RICHARD: Why not him?

BENOITE: Because ours is the brightest room in the house. It's always been the most cheerful. You'd think you were in the garden. And spring is coming. Soon, the buds will be swelling with juice. The lady next door has put up her awnings. Tomorrow, I'm going to do mine. In a couple of weeks, he'll be able to look out the window and see the first crocuses in bloom.

RICHARD: There must be other crocuses in the neighborhood.

FERNAND: Let's take it slowly, now. Careful. I can smell trouble! I'm out in the world, traveling the highways and byways sniffing things out like a truffle hound, looking for rare objects in one town so I can resell them in another. I turn old things into antiques, I sleep in hotels where the smell of frying onions wakes me at six a.m. And through wind and rain, whether there are

cows at the side of the road or not, I always chug my way home...
And then one fine day, before I've even had my breakfast, I'm
told that some stranger is going to live in my bedroom, I'm
treated like a doormat! So, Benoîte, let's forget the crocuses for
a minute, and let's hear you tell me straight out why I'm supposed to sleep for a whole month...

CAMILLE: More or less...

FERNAND: ...in a cramped little room where you store preserves
and geraniums...

CAMILLE: ...no ventilation.

BENOITE: No ventilation?

CAMILLE: The window's been papered over. You'll have to tear
the wallpaper off to get it open!

BENOITE: A bedroom, Fernand, is for nighttime, nighttime is
for sleeping. Your dreams are your own, you can have them anywhere. Preserves are very comforting. The geraniums will
soon go back out to the garden, like they do every year. And if,
in the wee hours of the night, you feel like chatting to me about
accounts or about eighteenth-century sugar bowls, one room is
as good as another!

FERNAND: A good thing I tell you about figures and sugar bowls!

BENOITE: Accounts done at night are never correct.

FERNAND: Tsk.

BENOITE: I did explain the whole thing to you in detail last night.

FERNAND: You explained the whole thing with no details. Is it
Chloe's future fiancé?

CHLOE: No, Papa. And he never will be.

FERNAND: (*to Camille*) Is he a political refugee? (*To Richard*) A criminal who's really innocent? (*To Benoîte*) A young runaway—and what if his family comes after us?

A brief pause.

CHLOE: He's a friend, Papa. That's what's important.

CAMILLE: Fine. And when's he arriving?

BENOITE: (*to Chloe*) When's he arriving?

CHLOE: Whenever you want. Tomorrow. This evening.

RICHARD: (*looking under the table*) Maybe he's here already?

FERNAND: In other words, it's all decided!

BENOITE: If we don't look before we leap, what are eyes for?

FERNAND: Where does this young man come from?

BENOITE: If someone's drowning, you don't ask to see his passport, do you, before you throw him a rope?

FERNAND: I'm beginning to feel like someone who's just flunked the exam to become a cop. (*The children chuckle. A pause.*) So, aside from "direst need," just what's the reason for his moving in?

BENOITE: What does he have? (*A pause.*) He's got nothing. Nothing at all. Precisely nothing.

FERNAND: No family?

CHLOE: No one. He's alone in the world. No father, no mother, no aunt, no brother, no cousin, no tutor. Not even a dog. Nothing.

CAMILLE: No friends?

CHLOE: Yes. Me. You, if you want to be.

BENOITE: *(to Fernand)* Could anyone be more an orphan?

FERNAND: There are orphanages for orphans.

BENOITE: Totally without resources.

RICHARD: And I suppose I have resources?

BENOITE: Confused. Lost.

FERNAND: Did your father work for years fixing up this place — that was just like a Turkish henhouse— just to make a home for the first stranger who happened to show up? How old is he?

CHLOE: I don't know—twenty, twenty-three, twenty-four.

FERNAND: No one's an orphan at *that* age. She doesn't know how old he is! (*To Benoîte*) Does she even know him, or did she just meet him on the bus?

Benoîte looks at him and shrugs her shoulders.

FERNAND: I'm being treated like someone's stray dog today.

BENOITE: You can say no. There's still time. But we'll never be the same family afterwards.

CAMILLE: It's a trap, Mother.

RICHARD: Or blackmail?

CHLOE: All he has is what we can give him.

An emotional silence. But the question is not settled yet.

FERNAND: Before he decided to take over my bed he must have been living somewhere?

CHLOE: In a very nice building in a very good neighborhood—cathedral windows, carpeting on the stairs. He had a room on the top floor, in the attic, no heat, no water, the bathroom two flights down.

FERNAND: At his age, which I don't know, I lived on the top floor. The mice used to eat my socks and puke them up the next day, and my john—more like an outhouse, it was—was way down in the courtyard.

BENOITE: You always have to outdo everybody!

FERNAND: Couldn't he pay his rent?

CHLOE: He had a scholarship. They've cut it off.

FERNAND: Why?

Chloe makes a gesture indicating ignorance.

BENOITE: I'll talk to the Mayor about it.

CHLOE: Mother!

BENOITE: Oh, yes... Good Lord, I was forgetting...

CAMILLE: What were you forgetting, Mother?

BENOITE: (*quickly, to avoid answering*) Does he have to be on a diet?

FERNAND: Oh, no! My room gone, and now yogurt at every meal!

CAMILLE: What's he like, physically?

CHLOE: Nice...very thin.

CAMILLE: (*who is on the plump side*) Another skinny one. What's he called?

CHLOE: Joseph.

CAMILLE: Like Stalin.

CHLOE: He had an uncle he was very fond of. He's gone.

FERNAND: I've got an uncle who's gone too. But I'm not going to move in with the neighbors. Benoîte, you say he's in dire straits. Just what do straits consist of nowadays?

CHLOE: He's got kind of a long neck, graceful.

FERNAND: Oh? So what?

CHLOE: Nothing. I was just telling you...while we're waiting...

A brief pause.

RICHARD: While we're waiting for him to ring the bell?

FERNAND: He's not Chinese by any chance?

CHLOE: No. Why?

FERNAND: There seems to be some kind of threat in the air. The grandmother you didn't know—good peasant stock from the coast—used to say that when a certain south wind blew over a family every member of it would change. The son who used to hang around in bars would suddenly begin to pull up sugar beets and potatoes and things that can be pulled up. The daughter who'd been had by everyone in the village would go into a convent; the mother, a good woman, would start setting fires to haystacks and the dog would stop biting the postman.

RICHARD: And the cows?

FERNAND: They'd watch the father bringing home his second-hand goods, the secondhand goods that support them all.

BENOITE: (*without malice*) And which my salary pays for.

FERNAND: Does he have a profession?

CHLOE: He studies.

FERNAND: Another one with two left hands!

CHLOE: He's learning carpentry. He's a working-class boy.

FERNAND: There's no question of asking him to pay rent, of course... And you can't put a price on a bedroom like ours. I suppose you couldn't find anyone we knew *less well* even if you looked!

BENOITE: No friend of Chloe's can really be a stranger.

FERNAND: You and Chloe are like birds sitting on your branches singing happily away at the top of your voices to drown out the sound of the woodsman below who's busy chopping down your tree.

BENOITE: Listen, Fernand. All our bills are paid up. We don't make a fortune, but we live comfortably. One of our daughters is in school, the other one in construction, our son hasn't yet found his niche...but that's just a question of time. We've all got our health. In the summer we go camping with the Lamberts. We're all tan until October. The cat's going to have kittens...

FERNAND: I know.

BENOITE: Your niece is going to marry a nice German boy, kind of into music, like all Germans, never any Nazis in the family, we can put off having the house painted until summer, Felicia, our turtle, that we thought had gone off in a snit, has come back, your mother's mood is greatly improved, especially where you're concerned...

FERNAND: Twenty years of trial and error...

BENOITE: After forty-eight payments that we'll hardly feel we'll own a set of Encyclopedia—that was supposed to be a surprise but it's too late now—the lady next door is a bit strange but she's a good neighbor all the same, I don't know how to play the piano, I've always regretted that, my mother used to say that the piano hadn't been invented for the likes of us, but that's all right, I've got my Glenn Gould cassettes...

FERNAND: Tsk. (*To Benoîte and the others*) And just what are you getting at now...?

BENOITE: I was thinking that...

FERNAND: Because once you've finished paying off what you owe and are lucky enough to have a niece who's marrying a German, it's the custom to offer your bed to the first person who comes along?

BENOITE: So, I thought that if this young man, alone in the world with nothing, forsaken by all, has happened to appear, to enter our lives, it's because he is in some way a solution to a long–standing problem.

FERNAND: Your mother turns into a mystic and nobody says a word? (*He rises as if to leave.*)

CHLOE: That's not all, Papa.

FERNAND: They used to say that you should never say you were happy out loud, for fear of making the Gods jealous...will we find we have to speak softly if he comes?

BENOITE: (*laughing*) We may.

FERNAND: Well then, open the door by all means, let's throw up the windows, let the bad luck in! Let it rip down the curtains, flood every room, let it empty our plates and destroy all our keepsakes and photographs.

BENOITE: *(laughing)* But why should that happen?

FERNAND: Because that's how bad luck is: it likes to punish those who pretend that winter feels like spring.

BENOITE: We once promised each other that we'd stay broad-minded and try looking at things beyond our limited territory...

FERNAND: Not as far as Greenland.

BENOITE: The third time we met, I remember, you told me...

RICHARD: Oh no, please! Not your private life...

BENOITE: You told me, "I'd like to have six children with you."

CHLOE: Mother! Didn't that scare you?

CAMILLE: You were right to stop halfway!

FERNAND: I was naive. And I didn't know how to count...

BENOITE: There's something so deeply emotional, so vivid, about happiness, it's best to hand it out...

FERNAND: Oh, come on!

They all look at each other. What next? Silence.

CHLOE: Mother, something's missing, I think.

BENOITE: Yes, Chloe, I know.

FERNAND: It's like a film where they've skipped a reel.

RICHARD: It's more like they've added one.

BENOITE: Why shouldn't we give, when we can?

FERNAND: What's got into you, Benoîte? We can't look after every other person in the world. There are too many of them, too many other people; they're everywhere, Benoîte! Endless numbers of other people!

BENOITE: So, ask a question, Fernand.

FERNAND: When you talk to me in that tender voice, something dangerous is on the way.

BENOITE: Go ahead, Fernand. Calmly, like you know how to do.

FERNAND: (*carefully, with thought*) ...Why him?

BENOITE: There! Thank you, Fernand. You've understood. Will you repeat your question, please?

FERNAND: I know you still love me. "Why him?"

BENOITE: (*taking a deep breath*) Because he's going to die.

> *Different reactions. Fernand jumps up. The silence reflects the import of her words.*

CAMILLE: Well, Mother, *that* got our attention.

FERNAND: He's...he's going to die?

BENOITE: Yes, Fernand.

FERNAND: (*looking around for moral support*) He's going to die? Does he know? Why is he going to die?

> *He exits swiftly.*

CHLOE: Is he angry?

BENOITE: He's upset.

RICHARD: He's got a reason to be.

BENOITE: He's a sensitive man.

RICHARD: One of your ideas, Chloe?

CHLOE: An idea of dire need.

CAMILLE: Are they sure?

CHLOE: The diagnosis is positive.

RICHARD: What disease is it?

CHLOE: It's got a name that's impossible to remember. Some dreadful thing that medical science can't cure for the moment.

RICHARD: A virus?

CHLOE: No, nothing like that. Last year, during school vacation, he had a job in a factory where they were experimenting with some new household product.

RICHARD: Shit! Dying for pots and pans.

CHLOE: There were thirty of them in the same workshop. Now there are only five.

CAMILLE: It was a sun–drenched morning.

RICHARD: Have you gone to bed with him?

CHLOE: Poor guy!

CAMILLE: I don't think I have enough courage to face it!

BENOITE: I know it's going to be hard.

CAMILLE: What are you getting us into, Mother?

FERNAND: (*returning*) Excuse me, I needed a large glass of water... What is it? Is he wounded? Is he bleeding?

BENOITE: He's ill.

FERNAND: You're going to think I'm a real pig: is he contagious?

CHLOE: No, Papa. I'd never have put you at such risk.

FERNAND: I don't think I'm brave enough for anything.

BENOITE: You stay just as you are, Fernand.

FERNAND: One of the family, that I could manage. But death —the unknown—in a stranger's body, that's a lot to ask at one time. Just imagining someone in my bed, going through what I'll be going through in a few years...tsk tsk tsk.

BENOITE: Come now, Fernand, you're young!

FERNAND: And so is he!

RICHARD: So what we're really doing is scuttling a ship just to save a fish.

CAMILLE: Not even save him. To watch him suffocate on the sand.

RICHARD: Why not the hospital? We could go to visit him...

CHLOE: They had to discharge him: they can't do anything for him.

    Silence.

BENOITE: So now you know. It wasn't easy.

FERNAND: Once, I saw a ten-storey building collapse, suddenly, just like a fat woman collapsing into a chair. (*Silence.*) You never should have left the Party, Benoîte.

BENOITE: What's the Party got to do with it?

FERNAND: Everything. Your dad was a farmer. Mine cleaned railroad cars. Since we both managed to do more with our lives, we can't complain. But you're still determined to accommodate the whole working class in your bed, while the working class has flown off to paradise. One lone sick young man isn't enough, Benoîte. All of suffering mankind is counting on you. We'll get our tent and pitch it somewhere, somewhere in the world where men are really suffering. People are caring for lepers. People are irrigating deserts. People are providing food in the slums. Let's not be stingy about it, while we're at it let's really go for it—nothing minor, let's go for the big one. No lukewarm hospitality, let's do it on a grand scale!

BENOITE: You can always say no. You haven't said anything to him yet, have you Chloe?

CHLOE: I haven't said anything to him.

FERNAND: Let's leave death to the dying. Death belongs to each of us, individually, alone. We're going to take in this young man as if he were a package being checked at a railroad station! If I were alone, sick and poor, I'd go off into the woods to die all by myself, in a hollow tree. Tsk tsk tsk.

CHLOE: Papa, you're talking like someone who's not alone, who's loved. What we can do for him is give him the only tenderness he'll ever have had in his whole life.

   Silence.

BENOITE: Indecision has always worked against generosity.

RICHARD: If you ask my advice, I'll tell you that it doesn't matter to me. So long as I can keep my own room.

CAMILLE: A young man is coming. He's bringing death with him. We squeeze a little closer together around the table. We make room for him. And life is still supposed to go on as usual?

CHLOE: What's that supposed to mean, in plain words?

CAMILLE: I'm not ashamed of having second-rate feelings: I'm scared.

CHLOE: What are you scared of?

CAMILLE: I'm scared of being scared. And a little more scared every day.

RICHARD: We just mustn't get attached to him, that's all.

BENOITE: Fernand?

FERNAND: ....

BENOITE: What have we decided?

FERNAND: Your wings are very large, Benoîte. Some day they'll hold you back.

BENOITE: You don't agree?

FERNAND: Or worse, you'll grow tired of them.

BENOITE: And?

FERNAND: But you're Benoîte.

BENOITE: What does that mean?

FERNAND: It means that we're going to sleep in the room with the geraniums.

BENOITE: (*beaming at them all*) Good. (*Still beaming*) It's crazy, how tired I feel all of a sudden.

RICHARD: This isn't the time, Benoîte.

BENOITE: Was I wrong?

RICHARD: I'll introduce you to Cliff Richards. He shares your perverse tendencies: he supports the third world.

CHLOE: Cliff Richards?

RICHARD: Chloe, why don't you give us a little?

And, in English, he begins to sing one of the singer's popular numbers.

CAMILLE: Starting tomorrow, you'll have to put a damper on Cliff Richards.

BENOITE: No, no; we'll live as we always do. If we feel like singing, we'll sing. We won't forget birthdays or anniversaries. And we'll laugh. That's the gift we'll give him: a warm happy family, with him a part of it. Right, Fernand?

FERNAND: Some day, I'm going to clip those wings. It'll be more practical for the whole family.

CAMILLE: (*imitating her father*) Tsk tsk tsk. It's like being in an old poem by old Victor Hugo.

WITH OPEN EYES

Night. Joseph is walking about the house like a sleepwalker. Chloe enters.

CHLOE: Can't you sleep?

JOSEPH: I sleep with my eyes open, it's better that way. (*Brief pause.*) And you, in the middle of the night?

CHLOE: (*tenderly*) I'm watching over you.

JOSEPH: Maybe someone will show up to tell me that it was all just a test of my courage and patience... Or maybe I'm really five years old and lost in a crowd. They're going to find me and I'm going to start to live a real life.

CHLOE: Are you tired?

JOSEPH: I often hear a sound...always the same one...a sound like paper being crumpled...

CHLOE: I dreamed that we were living on an ice floe, you and me... I was afraid because you were swimming in the sea, through huge icebergs...

JOSEPH: That's what I am doing...

CHLOE: I'm here.

JOSEPH: I know.

CHLOE: Beside you.

JOSEPH: Yes.

CHLOE: I think about you all the time.

JOSEPH: Not all the time, please; not all the time.

CHLOE: That should make you happy...

JOSEPH: That's another thing. (*Brief pause.*) Every evening—it's
what keeps me from sleeping—I have the same vision: I see a
huge double door, high as a three-storey house... Silently, the
doors swing open, behind them there's a bank of fog, fog so
thick that you can't see a thing. I move forward. I don't want to,
but I "must." I have an appointment to keep. Then, just as I
begin to cross the threshold, the fog begins to creep slowly
into the room, and I start to tremble...

CHLOE: When you're frightened, call me... I'll come...

JOSEPH: Don't do that...I might forget to die...

CHLOE: If you want *my* opinion, that's not going to happen. The
others, I can imagine all of them laid out on their beds, their
eyes closed, silent. Even my father and mother. Even Camille
and Richard, who're young—it's easy for me to imagine them
sleeping the sleep of eternity. But you, with you I can't see it at
all. So it's not going to happen.

JOSEPH: How will it be? Will I fix my eyes carefully on a certain
point and all of a sudden I'll understand? Is that what you think
it's like?

CHLOE: It's not going to happen to you.

JOSEPH: Once, on the bus, I almost threw my arms around a
woman.

CHLOE: Because she was beautiful?

JOSEPH: No more so than anyone else. It was such a fine day. The
town was actually glittering, like a jeweler's window. And I was so
happy to be alive that it just seemed to overflow, and this woman,
she was so alive, too... Now... I tell myself that I must have done
something really bad that I can't remember. At my age, death has
to be some kind of punishment. (*Pause.*) Will the sun die too?

CHLOE: They say it will.

JOSEPH: So it will have to pass through the double doors too... But it won't rot away...

CHLOE: (*taking his left hand*) Look at your long life line. (*She kisses his palm.*) I'll never forget you.

JOSEPH: Your memory will do that for you...it'll have plenty of time.

CHLOE: If it *does* happen to you, I'll be right beside you. You won't see me, but you'll hear me speaking to you. I'll be there. But it isn't going to happen to you.

JOSEPH: Swear.

CHLOE: I swear.

JOSEPH: On the head of...

CHLOE: On my own. That's still the one that means the most to me.

JOSEPH: Okay.

CHLOE: Am I being any help?

JOSEPH: Yes... Don't grow up too much.

CHLOE: So we each have a duty: I won't grow up too much and you... you'll "refuse."

JOSEPH: At night I seem to hear children in the street calling, "Mother."

CHLOE: Every night?

JOSEPH: Not every night. But what are they doing, those children, out so late at night? I'd never have thought it would make me feel so unhappy, so spiteful, just hearing people's footsteps hurrying home in the evening, their heads filled with plans, thinking up bits of life...

CHLOE: (*carefully*) What can I do?

JOSEPH: Nothing.

CHLOE: What would you like?

JOSEPH: To live. Just to live. Or not to have been born.

CHLOE: The disease hasn't made any visible progress...

JOSEPH: It's lying in wait. *It's* the crumpled paper. It's going to wrap me up. Sometimes, I can feel its breath on the nape of my neck. My father came up with another way of leaving the earth. He wasn't sick, he didn't have an accident. But one day he knew that the time had come.

CHLOE: How?

JOSEPH: You don't like anything any more: not the movies, not your friends, not swimming, not motorcycles. So you give a big party to say goodbye to your friends, your family. And when you feel a big frozen emptiness in your chest, you know it's time: you open the window and you fly away. Up, up into the air. But beforehand, you've arranged a time with those you love. And every evening or every morning, at the time you've arranged, you fly over the house. So the living wave to you, with their hands or they use some bright–colored cloth. And the young person who's dead flies off again until the next day...

CHLOE: And that happens forever and ever?

JOSEPH: No.

CHLOE: Until his loved ones die too?

JOSEPH: It happens until the day the ones he loves forget to open the window. Only once. One single time, and it's over forever. That's how my father died: they forgot the time.

CHLOE: I'd never have forgotten to open the window.

JOSEPH: Sometimes, night falls very quickly. (*Pause.*) I went into this library, trying to pretend to myself that I was a student. You were working there, your head in the dictionary. And on your shoulder there was a little curl that kept bobbing up and down, like a bee.

CHLOE: You watched me.

JOSEPH: Everything was new, then. I had so many thoughts. And then time began to rush by. To rush me... (*He laughs his own particular laugh.*)

CHLOE: Have you guessed how I feel about you?

JOSEPH: I think so.

CHLOE: Are you happy?

JOSEPH: Yes. And no.

CHLOE: Yes?

JOSEPH: Yes, because it's you. And no, because it's me.

CHLOE: Hold me.

JOSEPH: No. I'd burn up like a wheat field!

CHLOE: You'd burn up...

JOSEPH: You make me hope. And that's not recommended in my condition.

CHLOE: And I say it is.

JOSEPH: Don't give me something I've already lost.

CHLOE: If you let yourself be caught, I'll never console myself.

JOSEPH: Other people will. There's this solidarity among people... Tell me, your mother, isn't she what they call an idealist?

CHLOE: You could say that...

JOSEPH: And how old are you, really?

CHLOE: Really, I'm almost sixteen...

JOSEPH: You told me seventeen.

CHLOE: Oh, but that was a long time ago...

JOSEPH: Why are you smiling?

CHLOE: I'm thinking of the moment when I'll tell you I love you.

ACT II

A NIGHT OF CONFUSIONS

The entire family. They may be drinking coffee or tea. Fernand has just returned home. He is wearing his hat; his suitcase is beside him on the floor.

FERNAND: So I get to the place, I set out my stock. I'd got up with the sun. And the weather—it was like an oven. On the stroke of nine, this really good–looking woman showed up. I played it cool, I didn't go right over. You mustn't be too eager to sell something. And all of a sudden her eyes nearly fall out of her head and she starts yelling and pointing—she was wearing gloves— at a really good Eastern musical instrument, a real treasure, saying it used to belong to her mother, that it's a family heirloom, that it was always supposed to come to her, that it'd been stolen and that she was going to call the police, tsk, tsk, tsk...! I stay calm. I describe her mother to her: very short white hair, blue eyes, accent. I tell her: "I've got her phone number, you can call her." Tsk...tsk...tsk. So then she starts to cry. She feels like she's going to faint, she says, and she almost falls into my cut–glass pitchers. I prop her up, I say, "Sometimes, you know, people are short of cash..." Then she cries even harder. So I offer her some coffee.

BENOITE: You left the stand?

FERNAND: I had my thermos. (*A short pause. No one seems interested in the rest of the story.*) And what's been going on here?

CAMILLE: Not much.

RICHARD: A friend of mine just killed himself.

FERNAND: Why?

RICHARD: For public consumption, nobody knows. But I happen to know he was in love with a married woman, he'd asked her to run away with him and she'd refused.

FERNAND: How old was he?

RICHARD: Seventeen.

BENOITE: You never told us about that.

CAMILLE: We have all the suffering we need right here.

FERNAND: How did he do it?

RICHARD: He hanged himself with a scarf she'd given him.

FERNAND: Good Lord! In my day we didn't commit suicide so often.

RICHARD: The worst thing is that he died a virgin. When we used to talk about traveling, or later on, he would always say: "Don't be in such a hurry, pal, don't be in such a hurry." He always wanted to be a pilot. He took off too soon.

BENOITE: Is this little René?

RICHARD: No.

BENOITE: Oh! You had me frightened.

RICHARD: Because René's suicide would be so much worse than my friend's? I wanted to give a little concert for him, by the grave, but his mother didn't like the idea. The old fart didn't even cry. She couldn't even pretend to. I'd have pushed her in after him, but my friend wouldn't have appreciated her company.

> *He blows into his harmonica, playing a melancholy tune. Everyone is a little bored... "absent."*

FERNAND: Well, kids, the art market is worse than ever. I poke around in attics, junk stores, at farms with mud up to the second floor. No one has anything in their attics any more—nothing but plastic junk. And nowadays farmers know the precise value of that old hutch they've stuck out in the barn to age so that they can pretend it's a real antique. And at estate sales they'll try to sell you an old cracked bowl for some ridiculous price because Napoleon is supposed to have used it as an ashtray. Some guy told me—just to show you how values have changed—that he saw somebody hand over a wad of bills as thick as a dictionary for some lamb-chop bones the Beatles were supposed to have chewed on. Tsk...tsk...tsk...

> *Benoîte suddenly raises her head and looks up at the ceiling. The others do likewise.*

FERNAND: (*without much real interest*) How's he doing?

BENOITE: For several days now he's been moving more slowly...

CHLOE: That's because Papa's slippers are too big for him.

FERNAND: You gave him my slippers?

RICHARD: The old ones.

FERNAND: They were still good. He doesn't ever leave our...his room?

BENOITE: He's too weak...

FERNAND: It's been three months...

CAMILLE: And eleven days...

RICHARD: And eleven nights...

FERNAND: I don't think he's changed a bit since he plunked himself down here with us...

BENOITE: You're never home. And when you are here, you don't look at him.

FERNAND: He never leaves his room.

BENOITE: He doesn't bother you!

FERNAND: So, let him bother us! Let him live among us! I'd rather have a man around than some kind of limpet!

BENOITE: He gets paler all the time!

CAMILLE: No paler than when he came.

RICHARD: He's pale like I am when I stay in bed.

BENOITE: I see him through a mother's eyes: I can tell.

RICHARD: He went out last night.

BENOITE: How do you know that?

RICHARD: I was on my way in; we passed each other in the garden.

BENOITE: In the dark of night...

FERNAND: Full moon!

BENOITE: (*to Richard*) How was he?

RICHARD: He was wearing jeans!

BENOITE: Well, don't any of you get too concerned about it!

FERNAND: That's just it — I *am* concerned! Ever since he came, our lives have fallen apart. And that room upstairs is as oppressive as a stuffed elephant.

BENOITE: You aren't going to say that you don't think he's awfully thin. Chloe?

CHLOE: ...Somewhere between thin and not actually skinny...

BENOITE: Going out on such a chilly night... Of course he was coughing this morning.

CAMILLE: It was me coughing.

BENOITE: You could have told us!

FERNAND: So let me tell you what happened next... Well...

BENOITE: What if we had a little party for him. (*Astonishment all round*) Just a little one, something quiet and old fashioned— a little champagne, something to munch on, maybe some dip and a few mushrooms...

RICHARD: Edible?

BENOITE: Maybe some bread pudding...a little piano music...some family slides...

CHLOE: Family slides?

BENOITE: We wanted to give him a family—we should act like one.

CHLOE: When he sees us in our bathing suits at the shore, or playing on our swing, or giggling around our birthday cakes, blowing out the candles...

FERNAND: Your mother will try to make him think he's taken all the pictures.

BENOITE: Yesterday morning, in the bathroom, he was singing in a cracked little voice...

CHLOE: Mother, his voice isn't cracked...

BENOITE: Well then, weak!

CAMILLE: If his voice is weak then I'm starting on Wagner tomorrow...

BENOITE: (*persistent, losing her temper*) Weak. Weak as a kitten! Take the cotton out of your ears! You seem determined to contradict me today. (*To Fernand*) You could take off your hat when you come home.

FERNAND: I might as well take off the whole head...

An ill–humored silence.

BENOITE: (*in an attempt to raise family spirit*) Come on, come on! Let's not let it get us down! I'm certainly not going to. Anything worth doing is worth doing well. It's like we've set out on an expedition to the Antarctic—it's only going to get harder and harder. We all know that. But we can't do it by halves. We've got to tackle the whole thing, head on. And if our journey over the ice frightens us, it's because we've forgotten how to look death in the face. In the old days people confronted it—not like a friend, but like an acquaintance. Your grandfather spent his last days in that room upstairs. There was never a question of our leaving him there alone. One of the children was always sent up to sleep with him, to let him feel the warmth of life right up to the end. And the child would sleep curled up against the old man. And downstairs, in the parlor, the others waited, playing cards or dominos, drinking mulled wine, telling ghost stories. And sometimes this would go on for two, three days. The child never feared death.

RICHARD: And later, the child who didn't fear death would be sent off to war and die in some wheat field with no warmth and no grandfather! Come on, Fernand, tell us the rest of it... You gave her some coffee out of your thermos...

FERNAND: Between two crying fits, she drank my coffee out of an antique cup, and when she went off to powder her nose I lent her an antique mirror...

RICHARD: And then you propositioned her!

FERNAND: Didn't have time to! Some client inquired about the price of a shaving bowl, and when I turned around what do you think I saw? Or rather, what I *didn't* see?! I *didn't* see my beautiful Eastern instrument, a genuine antique, or any crying woman either...

RICHARD: Equally genuine...

FERNAND: Tsk...tsk...both vanished.

BENOITE: A neat trick. Well done!

FERNAND: You think so too?

They all laugh. A sound is heard.

BENOITE: Shhh!

In unison, they all look up to the ceiling.

RICHARD: See how we've begun to live: now our ears are glued to the ceiling.

BENOITE: I'll go.

CAMILLE: He dropped a book.

BENOITE: He can't read any more.

CHLOE: Yes he can, Mother. He reads a lot.

RICHARD: Children change. So do parents. When I was twelve I asked you to give a home to that guy who played the saxophone near the school...

BENOITE: He was a tramp...

RICHARD: (*with meaning*) And just what is your description of a tramp?

CAMILLE: Chloe is "Chloe." That's her charm. She might have shown up with a crocodile. Oh, look at the darling crocodile! Quick, let's give it a bath in swamp water and a hot chocolate!

BENOITE: Maybe he's not well...

CHLOE: I'll go. (*She exits.*)

FERNAND: She's not in love, is she? That would be awful.

BENOITE: (*taken aback*) In love? She's just a little girl.

The other two laugh.

CAMILLE: The other day she was saying that she would never allow herself to be "entangled in an amorous relationship."

FERNAND: A bad sign! At her age children say exactly the opposite of what they want.

RICHARD: So your sobbing woman must have had an accomplice!

FERNAND: If you'd only come with me.

RICHARD: I don't like old junk.

FERNAND: It's not old junk, it's antiques.

RICHARD: I like things that are smooth, polished, all in one piece, without bumps or decorations, all one color...

FERNAND: You're talking about formica! And yet it's a wonderful job. You have to have taste, discernment, a gift of the gab, self–control...

CAMILLE: And a thermos!

FERNAND: (*dreamily*) Yes...a lot of men are into data process-
ing, robots, synthetic reality, electronics. I'm in search of the
delicate things in life...things that have stood the long test of
time. Of course, the future worries me too. But some thin china
cup with pale blue flowers from which a girl might once have
sipped, a thing like that restores my faith. And when they ask
the price, I tell them it's "on hold." I want to keep it by me for
a while longer.

> *They look at Fernand. This is a side of him of which they are
> unaware. Chloe returns.*

CHLOE: He's gone out.

FERNAND: He's always going out! He lives here just so he can go
out!

BENOITE: He's sick, he's not an invalid!

FERNAND: When a person is sick, like he's supposed to be, they
stay in their room or they give it back!

RICHARD: You're right. The situation is getting to be too much
for me too. Death is ugly, but at least it's clean. It cuts, it sepa-
rates, it slices off, but it's a clean cut, and you don't have an
entire family sitting around waiting for something they don't
even dare talk about, with Mother Courage at the helm... No,
it's getting to be too much! If it keeps up I'm going to go off
and do my military service!

FERNAND: My father used to say, "You can't whistle and eat oat-
meal at the same time."

BENOITE: Which means?

FERNAND: Which means that you have to be careful: if you're
weak enough to let heroism sit down to eat with you, then don't
try to keep the conversation restricted to food. It'll just be havoc.

BENOITE: You've got a nerve saying that! You're away for two weeks without coming home. You stay in hotels where the phone's always out of order...

FERNAND: I don't have the time to look after the telephone lines!

BENOITE: (*with vehemence, but not aggressively. They are a close couple.*) You don't have the time! And what about me, my friend, you think I have time, after I come home from work, to fill the washing–machine, to call the plumber who puts me on hold over and over again to repair the leak in the john, to take your shoes to the shoe repair, to sign a petition to save Frederic Chopin Square—which turns out to be three little trees and a bed of tulips, which is of course better than nothing! —, to see that the gas and electric bills are paid on time, to water the bonsai, to feed the cat who eats enough for two, to look for the engagement ring I lost, to write your aunt who's stuck in what is laughingly called a "rest" home where that's the last thing she's getting, to try to cheer up a friend who's about to have a serious operation, to call your mother who's always asking where she can get hold of you, to fill out the whole family's health–care forms, to find out how much a new vacuum cleaner will cost because ours doesn't vacuum any longer and just coughs up dust...

FERNAND: You lost your engagement ring?

RICHARD: I feed the cat lots of times!

BENOITE: ...to make a list of the things I have to buy the next day on my way home from work, before I have to call the plumber back...

CHLOE: Show me how to water the bonsai, Mother.

CAMILLE: You could have asked us to look for your engagement ring...

BENOITE: When women get married they don't marry a man, they marry a job. That's the catch.

FERNAND: Come on! Two international trade shows. The two most important second-hand shows of the year. Buyers *made* of marks and dollars!

BENOITE: And when the husband comes home he starts to teach us our manners and complains about "havoc".

FERNAND: Benoîte, with all your burdens, of which I'm well aware and with which I do try to help the best I can—my poor best—why did you have to add another one, one heavier than all the others?

BENOITE: Because it's not a burden.

Silence.

CAMILLE: Okay. There's a horror film playing at the Apollo. Richard and I will leave you to your heroism and havoc. Are you coming, Chloe?

CHLOE: No thanks. I'm going to bed. Good night. (*She exits.*)

RICHARD: *(to Fernand)* I can't even give a decent tip to some poor usherette who never sees the light of day.

FERNAND: (*taking some money from his pocket*) Will that do it?

RICHARD: Well, it'll take care of the tip!

CAMILLE: (*feigning fright*) What about the horror? (*Fernand holds out another bill.*) The horror thanks you... Oh, and we'll talk about the wedding later.

BENOITE: And please, Richard, before you go to the movies, change your socks...

RICHARD: Not for a horror film.

FERNAND: *(to Camille)* What wedding?

CAMILLE: (*makes a sign signifying "don't ask"*) ...Later...

> *Exeunt Richard and Camille.*

FERNAND: They're so frightened that they have to seek comfort in horror.

BENOITE: They're not frightened. They're healthy children.

FERNAND: And Chloe would rather go to bed?

BENOITE: She gets up early. They take attendance.

FERNAND: Camille gets up a lot earlier.

BENOITE: Camille is a workhorse.

FERNAND: And Richard?

BENOITE: To each his own. "And Richard?" Well, "And Richard?" Nothing. There. Nothing. That's clear.

FERNAND: Does he do it on purpose?

BENOITE: Of course he does. At the moment, he doesn't like to work. He's far more intelligent than we are. He's very good with his hands. He did the bathroom—it's all like new. He doesn't like to work. Work has not yet entered his mind. In fact, he's still playing marbles.

FERNAND: That's perfect. I've nothing to say. The boy quit school—all the teachers were zeroes. He's subscribed to *Science and Life*. He knows all about the galaxies and genetic engineering. But he's still playing with marbles. Tsk tsk tsk!

BENOITE: Someday, he'll find...

FERNAND: He'll find a job where he's paid without working? We must be the only people in the world who just let things fall apart all around them...and...who... (*Looks up at the ceiling.*)

BENOITE: Fernand, why not just come out and say you're proud of us?

FERNAND: Proud? More like peeved! Listen, Benoîte, what do you think's going to become of us...you...the children...your mother...your sister...tsk, tsk, tsk.. Because in the end – forgive me, you're going to say I'm being beastly—here we are, down here sitting underneath our bedroom, going around in our stocking feet, whispering like conspirators, stifling our laughter, stuck in a tunnel waiting for something that is supposed to happen and that never does... It's been five months now...

Pause.

BENOITE: Three...

FERNAND: Spiritually, it's been five...that we've all been prisoners of an unbearable situation. I'm worried about you all, let me tell you...a great deal more than I show...

BENOITE: Death will settle it. It always has. It always does.

FERNAND: What are you talking about! If this mysterious disease keeps dragging on, and dragging us after it, for months, for years—and what's to stop it?—then what are you planning on doing?

BENOITE: Nothing more. Nothing less. I've committed myself.

FERNAND: No. It can't go on like this. I'm walking on broken glass. The *insides* of my bones ache. My lungs are like mouse holes. I live on crumbs...

BENOITE: And your indigestion the other night?

FERNAND: From crumbs.

BENOITE: They told you it wasn't contagious.

FERNAND: It's not a question of contagious. It's a question of premonition. I can hear my death walking above my head: up there, in my bedroom, someone is rehearsing the last moments of my life, perfecting them.

BENOITE: You're crazy!

FERNAND: I'll deal with it by myself, I don't need a stand–in.

Benoîte bursts out laughing.

FERNAND: I wonder sometimes if you aren't a little bit crazy.

BENOITE: (*suddenly serious*) It's such a small thing, Fernand. There's always been blood on the ground... But today, when men slip in innocent blood, all they say is, "Aha! it's about time I had my shoes resoled."

FERNAND: And how will it be for him...in the end?

BENOITE: An immense fatigue...then a kind of paralysis...

FERNAND: Good Lord! What are we coming to?

BENOITE: And they say that in the final days the body becomes translucid...

FERNAND: Translucid... (*Brief pause.*) Haven't we taken on more than we can handle? I sleep more and more badly...

BENOITE: So do I. But that boy, now, I love him like one of my own.

Pause.

FERNAND: Oh la la la la la la la!

BENOITE: You're right, Fernand.

She exits. Fernand is alone, bemused, exhausted.

FERNAND: La la!

Benoîte reenters with a bottle of champagne and glasses.

BENOITE: It's not only for birthdays. It's also for days that are too hard. For the women and men we are turning into. For all we're leaving behind. For all the things we wanted to say. For the forgotten things. For old and future angers. For all we've been spared. Ah, Fernand! Fernand! We're together, and the syringa is going to have a lot more flowers than it did this time last year.

FERNAND: Translucid!

BENOITE: Drink.

Then, adopting the same posture, both become lost in thought.

FERNAND: I was young. It was the first time I'd gone to Italy. I didn't know what trompe–l'oeil meant, I didn't even know the term. It was the height of summer. I went into an abbey to cool off. There, in the old refectory, dark, with a smell of wax, I saw this long oak table set for a snack, with carafes of wine and plates of cakes. There were some fruit peelings on the floor, and I bent down to pick them up.... Well, the guardian was just waiting for me to try it, and he burst out laughing...

BENOITE: He was a farmer, astonishingly strong. I admired him so much: when I was a little girl I saw him bring a bull to its knees by grabbing its horns and forcing it down, a mad bull that was trying to get out of the field...

FERNAND: I've had other Italies...more beautiful, more sensual, crazier—and other abbeys too. In one of them, I remember, there was a tiled floor in trompe–l'oeil, and one of the tiles had a fake crack. Lots of visitors used to stumble over it without knowing why. I even saw a woman trip over the "broken" tile and fall...

BENOITE: My parents didn't like him, because when he was just a boy he'd joined the Party. But I liked him because he had. He helped that poverty-stricken village stay on its feet.

FERNAND: And one day—it was the sixth or seventh time I was in Italy, I loved Italy like a woman—I finally discovered that monastery where everything, absolutely everything, is an illusion: there are columns that only seem to be holding up the walls, there are stairways that seem to lead to long, unreal corridors, stone windows that seem to open onto skies full of clouds. In one of the rooms there's what looked like a huge well right in the center of the floor...

BENOITE: I'd kind of forgotten about the place where I grew up. And the uncle who knew how to tame bulls. I grew up. And when the time came, I joined the Party too.

FERNAND: The well seemed to be set level with the floor. Visitors liked making a game of it—men would push their wives towards the dark opening and they would pretend to be terrified and make funny noises. The guardians would laugh a lot...

BENOITE: When I went back one summer, that bad summer, the Little Father of the Peoples was no longer a good father. They'd discovered he was the worst of tyrants. And that strong farmer, I saw him crying, wiping his eyes with his big striped handkerchief all rolled up in a ball.

FERNAND: The women would make noises and the guardians would laugh. But that day something awful happened. A little girl of five disappeared. The monastery was searched from top to bottom. The friar who kept the door swore that no child had gone out, either alone or accompanied. The police came, but the search came to nothing.

BENOITE: One night he dug a deep hole in his vegetable garden. And in the morning we found him there, buried up to the neck. He threatened to kill anyone who tried to keep him from dying. And he would have. He died crying.

FERNAND: And later on, I heard that the room with the trompe–l'oeil well had been closed up.

A pause. Both of them "come back." They smile at each other.

BENOITE: (*pointing to the ceiling*) We were right, weren't we?

FERNAND: Even if we were, were we wise? (*Camille and Richard enter.*) Back already?

RICHARD: The film stank, the special effects were so–so, I could have done them myself in the kitchen. It was about a tribe of people who feed on human heads, but live ones, still warm...

FERNAND: Very interesting...

RICHARD: So they appeal to the high priests, who set out to find a special mushroom with the power to...

CAMILLE: We'll tell you the rest at breakfast tomorrow morning. Fernand, your niece called. She's getting married on the fifteenth. In Germany.

FERNAND: The fifteenth of...?

CAMILLE: This month.

FERNAND: That'll make a change for us. We'll fly.

BENOITE: Who'll go?

FERNAND: All of us, of course.

BENOITE: I won't. He can't be left alone.

FERNAND: What do you mean? It's my only brother, the only niece I've got, it's her first marriage...

BENOITE: We can't go to every wedding...

FERNAND: We're only talking about one.

CAMILLE: What can we say to them?

BENOITE: Tell them I'm ill.

RICHARD: Chloe hates ceremonies.

BENOITE: We can't leave a child like that to face such a thing!?

FERNAND: You see? We offer hospitality to a young man. We give him our warmth, our house, our garden, and he keeps us from attending a wedding.

CAMILLE: We asked for this young man. We'll find a solution.

RICHARD: The lady next door has always offered to help...

BENOITE: But we should stay with him to the end.

FERNAND: Do you think it's going to come in those three days?

BENOITE: Can anyone say it won't?

CAMILLE: Let's take him with us.

BENOITE: That's right! So that the blow will fall right in the middle of the ceremony!

FERNAND: And none of us speaks German!

　　　Joseph enters.

JOSEPH: Has something serious happened?

ALL: No, no...nothing...

BENOITE: No, Joseph, it's nothing.

JOSEPH: You all looked so worried, I was afraid...

Pause.

FERNAND: How are you feeling?

JOSEPH: I don't know... I can see that I'm causing you more and more trouble...

BENOITE: You're a part of the family...and we're here, with you.

JOSEPH: I know...

BENOITE: If this good weather holds, we'll have lunch in the garden tomorrow. Would you like that?

JOSEPH: Yes. Next year, this time next year, will the syringa and the roses be blooming...?

BENOITE: (*uneasily*) Probably.

JOSEPH: Yes... It will all go on...of course. Summer will follow summer. Year after year the trees will put out new leaves. The brass door knockers shaped like hands will still be polished and shiny, the warm sky won't change... And every winter the turtle will bury herself but still live. On the door of the house with the blue shutters the hand is wearing an engagement ring. I touched it, it was still warm. And in the rue de la Petite Armée couples will still kiss under the golden glow of the street lamps... Forgive me...I'm ashamed...it's difficult.

RICHARD: What about a game of chess...?

BENOITE: In the middle of the night?

RICHARD: Yes, but we'll light some more lights, Mother. He plays well, he's a real Karpov.

JOSEPH: To really play that game well you can't think of either the past or the future.

CAMILLE: Why don't you take us with you when you go out walking at night?

JOSEPH: I don't go far. This evening, to the Place Gutenberg, there was an impromptu dance...an accordion, drums, a violin player...

RICHARD: In honor of...?

JOSEPH: In honor of a woman who couldn't have a child—she cleans for the whole neighborhood and everyone likes her— she's just had twins. Her husband's a black. A woman asked me to dance...

CAMILLE: Young?

JOSEPH: Young–ish.

RICHARD: What was it like?

JOSEPH: It was all right...but...I stopped in the middle of it. It suddenly occurred to me that I should leave your house.

BENOITE: Why?

JOSEPH: This waiting for what's going to happen is getting long for me, but even longer for you, because I can feel that you're trying not to think about it...

BENOITE: And where will you go?

JOSEPH: Fine weather is coming. A person can live outdoors.

BENOITE: So, we'll just have to tie you to the bed.

JOSEPH: On the way back here I remembered all sorts of things I'd forgotten. I remembered myself as a child when I couldn't tie my shoe laces. I remembered that my first movie was a Chaplin film and that I cried because of the dog. That later on I came home with a dog I said was lost—of course it wasn't true—and that that had earned me a good spanking. That one day, in a park, a man had stared at me in such an odd way that I'd blushed... I'm telling you all these things...I don't know why...

CAMILLE: The twins, did you see them?

JOSEPH: Yes. One is all white and the other one's all black.

CAMILLE: Do they look alike?

JOSEPH: They're like day and night. (*They laugh quietly.*) The little violinist played very well...

Chloe enters. She looks at the others, but speaks to Joseph.

CHLOE: Aren't you feeling tired?

JOSEPH: You've got to speak to your parents. (*He exits.*)

CHLOE: What's the matter?

BENOITE: (*tenderly*) Nothing, dearest... Nothing. (*Chloe exits.*) To me, he looks like an angel.

CAMILLE: Think, Mother. Think.

FERNAND: And the wedding?

CAMILLE: What *I* think is that we haven't got enough trouble already. It's all timid, skimpy, mean... It's like the entire ocean were calling out for help, and we've managed to care for a drop of water. A third of the world's children are being tortured and forced into prostitution, another third are dying of hunger and the rest are either amusing themselves by playing video games or sitting bored to death in front of their TV sets. Today's Monday—on Saturday there will be 250,000 fewer children in the world. Two hundred and fifty thousand fewer, by the time

Richard and I go to see the new horror film at the Apollo.

BENOITE: I don't have room to take in 250,000 children a week.

CAMILLE: Saint Martin gave only half his cloak to a beggar and they both died of cold. Give the whole coat or keep it for yourself. Anything else is amateur... I've got to tell you, Mother: Yesterday Chloe and I had a long talk with Joseph. He told us that he was feeling much better.

BENOITE: Ah! That's why he seems so worried. It's what they call a remission.

FERNAND: And our wedding in Wurtemberg?

Blackout.

WHAT'S HAPPENING TO US?

Night. Fernand and Benoîte meet, Benoîte carrying a glass and carafe of water.

BENOITE: I was so thirsty...

FERNAND: Me too.

BENOITE: The champagne...

FERNAND: Where did you get the water...

BENOITE: From the kitchen. Why?

FERNAND: The water in the bathroom comes from a spring...from the Alps..

BENOITE: Are you trying to make me laugh?

FERNAND: It was only a try.

> *Benoîte pours a glass of water, looking at him. She drinks and offers Fernand her glass.*

FERNAND: Can't you sleep?

BENOITE: No.

FERNAND: Oh no? I wanted to say good night to you...and you were already out like a light.

BENOITE: (*evasively*) Ah... that's unusual.

FERNAND: What's happening to us?

BENOITE: I don't know... I don't know yet.

FERNAND: Why don't we make love any more?

BENOITE: (*with difficulty*) I feel as though I'd been frozen...

FERNAND: I know.

BENOITE: Perhaps...perhaps the thought of death is killing the love we used to hold in our arms...

FERNAND: And further down as well...

BENOITE: The body never tells everything it's thinking.

FERNAND: Are we going to go beyond the limits?

BENOITE: When things get too difficult you just have to imagine that someone you love is looking at you very hard...

FERNAND: Who loves us enough to look at us now? We never laugh any more. We barely breathe. Camille goes around making odd pronouncements. You lose your engagement ring. And you want someone to look at us...

BENOITE: We're going to begin to reproach him for still being alive.

FERNAND: How did he manage not to have any family at all?

BENOITE: He's not an orphan any longer. We're here.

FERNAND: We won't save him, and we're losing ourselves. And you just go chugging off into the future, like you've always done, like some locomotive...

    He holds out his glass and she refills it.

BENOITE: Don't worry. I'll come back.

FERNAND: I do worry. You turn into a different woman from one moment to the next, and the house seems to get smaller and smaller. (*A pause.*) What about our vacation?

BENOITE: We'll go for winter sports.

FERNAND: And I'll fall down, like I always do.

BENOITE: Do you find me a little...sterile...these days?

FERNAND: A bit like a statue in a park. And yet, what a wonderful summer it's been! It'll be years before we have such weather again! Before we leave, I'm going to string the hammock up between the two birches.

BENOITE: The cat's had her litter.

FERNAND: How many?

BENOITE: Two.

FERNAND: We'll keep them.

Pause.

BENOITE: (*in a low voice*) Fernand...I hope...I hope the end is near.

FERNAND: Tomorrow you'll wear the red dress you bought yourself for my birthday.

BENOITE: Are we a good couple?

FERNAND: Yes. But we mustn't let the sheets on our bed get much colder.

JUST HOLD OUT

Night.

JOSEPH: Tell your parents to throw me out.

CHLOE: They like you.

JOSEPH: They didn't know me.

CHLOE: They knew me.

JOSEPH: Hold me.

CHLOE: (*putting her arms around him*) There.

JOSEPH: Do they talk about me?

CHLOE: All the time.

JOSEPH: I could have been born here. When I came, I had nothing. And I'm going to lose it all. Why me, Chloe? Everyone else lives, breathes, makes appointments, I'm the only one who's dying. Only me.... Day and night, someone is whispering into my ear. It's not leaving that's sad: it's not knowing what's going to happen afterwards...how things are going to turn out. The things they're going to invent.... You'll never hear birds, or trains in the night.... When life goes, the whole world follows it. Death is a kind of betrayal.

CHLOE: Last night I looked for you all over the house.

JOSEPH: I went to sit in front of the door of my old room.

CHLOE: To...?

JOSEPH: To get used to my absence.

CHLOE: Stop.

JOSEPH: Don't be too unhappy, Chloe. Sometimes, I feel so much better that I stand in front of the mirror and I say: "*That's* the person who's going away, *I'm* staying." (*Pause.*) Once I was three years old, seven, twelve.... And all those children are going to go away too...holding each other by the hand...all off to get lost in the forest...

CHLOE: Isn't there anything left of your family?

JOSEPH: My father's in an asylum.

CHLOE: Has he been there long?

JOSEPH: I was twelve...

CHLOE: Do you visit him?

JOSEPH: He still asks for his old coat.

CHLOE: Did he lose it?

JOSEPH: I always remember him in that old gray overcoat, almost worn through. He loved it like you love a pet. When his troubles began to get too much for him, he got it onto his head that his coat was sick, that he had to feed it. He used to share all his meals with it: every evening he'd set a plate of food underneath where it was hanging on a hook. I managed to get rid of the food. I was always hungry, I used to eat like a pig. But when I couldn't finish it all...well, there would be tears. And then, where he is now, they confiscated it.

CHLOE: Were there just the two of you?

Joseph doesn't answer.

CHLOE: Will he get well?

JOSEPH: (*with violence*) Go away! You don't understand a thing. You're one of those people who are able to see ahead. Go back to your bed, with its clean white sheets. Disease doesn't sleep in your arms. Go away. Go back to bed and dream: you've still got sixty years ahead of you!

CHLOE: Joseph, look at me. Nothing is going to happen. Do you hear me? Nothing is going to happen to you. Don't leave. Don't disappear. Just don't do it. Stand up straight. Don't turn around. Don't listen to that sound of paper being crumpled.... Be like marble, be steel. Shave every day. I'm holding you. You can't fall. In two months the cherries will be ripe. You'll climb up into the tree and I'll hand you up a basket to fill. Don't look at anything in the sky but the stars that concern you. For the rest, we'll see later.... If a dog comes up to you, speak to it softly, but don't bend down to pet it. That too, we'll see about later. If someone asks you for directions, pretend you're blind. If a child asks you questions, tell it you're expecting a wolf to show up any minute. Don't be afraid, nothing is going to happen. It almost did...but now it's over. The storm has passed. There's just the smell of wet grass. You just have to "hold on" a little. And soon we'll cross the line.

JOSEPH: And the big double door?

CHLOE: It's made of cardboard.

JOSEPH: And the fog?

CHLOE: It's dry ice, like in the movies. Some day we'll be on a beach...the sea will be high and crashing...I'll ask you not to go in swimming.

JOSEPH: But I will anyway.

CHLOE: I'll be afraid. When you come out of the water I'll lay my head against your wet back... I'll put my arms around you and clasp my hands over your chest. I can hear your heart under my hands. (*A pause.*) And we'll take a nap together. We'll lie down next to each other. The sun will travel across the ceiling.

JOSEPH: A fly will buzz against the blinds?

CHLOE: Of course. We won't sleep. And from downstairs, some-one will be calling us.

JOSEPH: Will we go down?

CHLOE: You tell me not to answer.

> *A pause.*

JOSEPH: And what is all that supposed to mean?

CHLOE: It means that if you believe me you'll see all the springs that are ahead of us, and all the summers too.

> *A pause.*

JOSEPH: And if I come out of this?

CHLOE: What's the first thing you'll "do?"

JOSEPH: I'll set out to cross the Hoggar desert...

CHLOE: Have a good trip, Mr. Joseph...

JOSEPH: I'll never be able to do without you...

CHLOE: In the desert?

JOSEPH: You beside me...dressed in blue.

THE GOUDELKAS

They all enter, each carrying bread – one a baguette, another a brioche, etc.

FERNAND: This isn't a family, it's a bakers' convention.

RICHARD: For once I was up early; I wanted to surprise you.

CAMILLE: It's enough of a surprise to find you out of bed.

BENOITE: Having all of you here for breakfast already makes it seem like a holiday.... Where's Chloe?

CAMILLE: She left a note. She's at a friend's house.

FERNAND: She's living more and more apart from us...

RICHARD: We managed to replace her at a moment's notice: I invited the lady next door.

BENOITE: What's got into you?

CAMILLE: *(to Fernand)* Some mysterious bond between them?...

FERNAND: It's the first time I've seen Richard holding a brioche...

The doorbell rings.

CAMILLE: There's Mrs. Ronsard now, our turtle–dove... "See, Mignonne, how doth the rose...."

Richard goes to the door. Mrs. Ronsard enters.

MRS. RONSARD: I've brought croissants—what a marvelous idea, really marvelous, because for me, really, breakfast is always the *most* important meal of the day, and you with that boy who's sick, upstairs, is he a cousin?

BENOITE: No, no.

MRS. RONSARD: Oh, really? Not related...it's really very *brave* of you all, when you're all just *swamped* with work—two jobs, the house, the garden, three children, a cat...

CAMILLE: *And* a turtle!

MRS. RONSARD: Oh, did it come back? Oh, yes, turtles are the only animals that can dig themselves up, is he an orphan, then, your young man?

FERNAND: That he is.

MRS. RONSARD: Well, it can happen to anyone. But I *do* admire you, I couldn't do it, I'd want to but I'd think twice about it, he's too far gone, but if you ever need me I'll be there, because life— well, that's life, if someone asks you, you've got to respond, life is nothing but toil, and toil is...

RICHARD: Toil is toil!

FERNAND: Richard, behave yourself!

MRS. RONSARD: And then after life, what is there, there's death! And *some* people will tell you that between life and the bitter end there's love. But what's love? Bread and butter... Only what they *don't* tell you is that the butter isn't *on* the bread but under it and if it melts in a warm embrace, the butter, I mean, is he in pain?

BENOITE: Not yet.

MRS. RONSARD: Well, that's something, anyhow, and then Richard dropped by to invite me, I wasn't really prepared to face the day, I'd hardly opened my eyes, I hope my cologne doesn't bother you, it's Carpathian Verbena.

RICHARD: And speaking of the Carpathians...

FERNAND: *(opening the newspaper)* What's been happening in the Carpathians?

MRS. RONSARD: Probably another war. My father used to say that war was all they *did* in the Carpathians.

RICHARD: The Goudelkas!

FERNAND: Don't know them. What about breakfast...we've invited the lady next door...

BENOITE: Richard, why did you mention the Goudelkas? (*To Fernand*) We met them last year at that museum...

RICHARD: There you are!

FERNAND: What do you mean, "There you are?"

BENOITE: Does it mean *here they are?*

RICHARD: You win, Benoîte.

BENOITE: They're coming?

RICHARD: It certainly looks like it to me.

FERNAND: Great! We'll have a great time!

BENOITE: Not necessarily.

FERNAND: Are they sick too?

BENOITE: We offered to put them up.

FERNAND: Why here?

BENOITE: Because hotels here are too expensive for folks from the East.

MRS. RONSARD: They didn't *have* to vote communist!

FERNAND: (*remembering*) Oh, no, oh no! What are we getting ourselves into now?

CAMILLE: The Goudelkas!

FERNAND: *(to Benoîte)* Your idea?

BENOITE: What do you mean, *my* idea! I'm not the foreman, I'm not an architect, or a movie director, or a map maker or a surveyor or a member of the general staff. *My idea!* What idea?

CAMILLE: Give them *my* room. I'll go stay with friends...

BENOITE: You've forgotten the size of your bed...

RICHARD: They can sleep on top of each other, lots of people do...

MRS. RONSARD: Since you've invited me for breakfast may I make so bold as to ask: what about *your* room?

BENOITE: Our sick friend is in it.

FERNAND: And we're sleeping among the geraniums!

MRS. RONSARD: Good lord, your own room! You can put the geraniums out, now, it's not going to freeze again, I could lend anything a person might need, even underclothes, even my umbrella, but not my bed, you really are a model family...

FERNAND: Yes, yes...I remember them now, very fine people, speaking our language, Benoîte, have you any idea...

BENOITE: Why am I always supposed to have the ideas? Can't you have one? We're both responsible for the Goudelkas, and I'm the one who's supposed to carry the whole load, families, surprises, plans, the phases of the moon, the Goudelkas and the Carpathians!

FERNAND: You're the one who's always inviting the entire world to sleep in our bed. (*To Richard, in order to divert Benoîte's anger*) And now you're opening our mail, are you!

RICHARD: I saw the stamp. I guessed. I wanted to spare you any sudden shock.

FERNAND: What language did they write in?

CAMILLE: In Carpathian!

FERNAND: Since when have you thought you could open our mail?

RICHARD: The envelope said "The Cormorans," I thought I was still one of the family.

FERNAND: You're not "The Cormorans," you're just one of them. When are they coming?

RICHARD: At the end of the month.

FERNAND: The same time as our wedding in Germany!

    The telephone rings; Benoîte goes to answer it.

MRS. RONSARD: Do you speak German?

FERNAND: No, but with my brother we can do without it.

MRS. RONSARD: I've known some people who spoke foreign, it was impossible to make them understand what they were trying to say...

CAMILLE: You could stay at a hotel... (*Benoîte returns.*) You can go to a hotel and leave them your room.

BENOITE: A room full of preserves for people who've been having trouble finding enough food for years now!

CAMILLE: You can load them up with food when they leave...

BENOITE: Offering hospitality to friends when there might be a sudden death in the house at any moment...

FERNAND: Who was that on the phone?

BENOITE: Your mother.

FERNAND: That was quick!

BENOITE: She offered to pay for our trip to Germany!

FERNAND: There you are: she "offered." A lot of good offering does! This is what we get for unbridled charity: a boy descends on us from nowhere, under sentence of death. He sleeps in our bed. He eats at our table. He's not a son, not an uncle, not a friend, he's not even the son of a friend, the friend of a friend. And instead of dying he shilly–shallies around. And then everything falls apart—no wedding at Wurtemberg, a brother and a niece left in the lurch, our friends from the East deported, a family that's going to the dogs...

BENOITE: We could just drag him out by the feet and leave him on the sidewalk...

RICHARD: (*to Mrs. Ronsard*) This isn't why I invented—I mean, invited—you...but you told me once that you always had an extra bedroom...

MRS. RONSARD: Yes, I call it the "emergency room," it was my husband's old office and as you know my husband left me but I still see my in–laws and you know—such a bore!—this is more or less the time of year they always come to visit, I would really have been more than happy otherwise...

FERNAND: It doesn't matter, Mrs. Ronsard.

MRS. RONSARD: But it does, yes it does, it does matter...

BENOITE: You're all looking at me as though it were up to me to keep everything running smoothly.

CAMILLE: No one's criticizing you, Mother. It's just that we're not used to thinking...

BENOITE: I'm not well. I ache all over! And it's getting worse. I'm going back to bed. I'll sleep on it. Yesterday I had a disagreement with my boss. Here we are a welfare office and he goes and slaps a poor kid who'd been waiting for two hours with his mother and had started to run up and down in the hallway... No, no! Before, I used to be able to hold my...

FERNAND: Before what?

BENOITE: Stop it, Fernand! You're like my boss... (*To the neighbor*) Excuse me, Mrs. Ronsard. (*She hands her bread to Camille.*)

MRS. RONSARD: No excuse needed.... But I will, of course, take it as offered...

FERNAND: *(to Richard)* You've always got such good ideas!

RICHARD: I didn't invite the Goudelkas!

FERNAND: Yes you did, and you told them to come too early.

He hands his bread to Camille and exits.

Chloe enters carrying a large round loaf of country bread.

CHLOE: I thought we might as well have a hearty breakfast...

RICHARD: Well, Mrs. Ronsard, you may not have a spare room, but you're entitled to one of your croissants anyway.

MRS. RONSARD: Some other time, when you need a room, I'll arrange something with the woman next door to *me*...she can always manage to put someone up...like me.

CAMILLE: (*who is now holding all the loaves of bread*) No, no...I like bread, yes, but...

Blackout.

ACT III

TEARS! TEARS!

Chloe runs in crying and throws herself into Benoîte's arms.

CHLOE: Mother, mother...

BENOITE: My darling, my child...

CHLOE: Listen...

BENOITE: You don't have to say anything...I understand.

CHLOE: No, no...

BENOITE: There are no words to express...what can't be changed.

CHLOE: It's not that...not that...

BENOITE: We've been living with this threat...for months...

CHLOE: Mother...I've got to tell you that...

BENOITE: We'll both cry for him, Chloe.

CHLOE: It's not that...

BENOITE: We'll never forget him.

CHLOE: Mother, let me tell you...

BENOITE: Did he suffer?

Chloe bursts out laughing.

BENOITE: Come now, calm down...my child be calm. From the very first day...we knew how it was going to end... But our knowing didn't make it any easier for us to bear it...that's true...

CHLOE: Mother, mother, cry with me...

BENOITE: I am, my child.

CHLOE: I must tell you...

BENOITE: I know, I know...

CHLOE: No, you don't...

BENOITE: We all felt as though he was one of us....

Chloe pulls away from her mother, calms down...

CHLOE: Please, Mother...

BENOITE: Come, we'll go see him... (*as suddenly Joseph enters, shirtless, resplendent in white pants. Benoîte cries out.*) Who...what...is it really you?

JOSEPH: It is. Your Joseph. Alive.

BENOITE: What do you mean, alive?

JOSEPH: More than alive. Free of death! Like Lazarus! (*He laughs.*) The dictionary doesn't have words to describe what I feel. (*To Benoîte*) Kiss me. (*They embrace.*) Can I call you Mother, now?

BENOITE: (*laughing, stammering*) Oh...but...it's a word that...

JOSEPH: Now that I've got my whole life ahead of me...I don't have a second to lose.

He exits, laughing.

BENOITE: Cured?

CHLOE: Yes, Mother.

BENOITE: Cured! But why that ghoulish joke?

CHLOE: (*laughing*) My tears were choking me...I couldn't get a word out...and you wouldn't listen to me...

BENOITE: He's cured?

CHLOE: You aren't happy?

BENOITE: Of course I am...

CHLOE: You're not overwhelmed...like I thought you'd be...

BENOITE: You expect me to change in a few seconds from grief to...

CHLOE: You see, you can't find the words...

BENOITE: What do you mean, I can't...

CHLOE: Grief...to joy! Joy, Mother.

BENOITE: Yes, that's it: joy. That's what I was going to say, if you'd just let me get it out.

CHLOE: So now cry, Mother, cry like I cried. Cry for joy!

BENOITE: (*almost angry*) I am crying!

CHLOE: Your eyes are dry.

BENOITE: People are different—I cry without tears.

CHLOE: Mother, he's saved!

BENOITE: I could tell that. What happened?

CHLOE: Well, for a month now, the doctors have all been wondering. And today they made it official. All his tests are negative. There's no longer any trace of the disease. Joseph is as good as the day he was born. Isn't it wonderful?

BENOITE: All the doctors who said...

CHLOE: All of them.

BENOITE: The same diagnosis?

CHLOE: Every one, without exception.

BENOITE: Do they have any explanation?

CHLOE: They don't explain. They just report.

BENOITE: Still, it's very strange to leave a sick person in such uncertainty...

CHLOE: He's not sick any more, mother, and there's no uncertainty. Either *our* love for him has triumphed over death, or...

BENOITE: He was mis–diagnosed.

CHLOE: Well, they'll never admit that. There were so many tests, so many examinations, X–rays, analyses...

BENOITE: But what if today's diagnosis is a mistake?

A pause.

CHLOE: Why do you say that, Mother? What are you trying to do?

BENOITE: I'm just trying to see clearly...where we stand...

CHLOE: It's simple. He's saved. He's not going to die.

BENOITE: Ah?!...

CHLOE: And *I* think that we're the ones who've saved him...

BENOITE: Don't get all mystical... He's cured because he was meant to be cured.

CHLOE: Oh, Mother, I didn't know a person could cry for joy. These tears are just as salty as the other ones, but how much sweeter they are. And him! He says that waking up in the morning is the most beautiful thing that's ever happened to him. He goes around touching things. He's talking to the crows that fly around the house. He keeps saying our names out loud. When he looks up at the sky, his eyes fill with tears.

Joseph enters carrying a tree, which he gives to Benoîte.

JOSEPH: And that's just the beginning...

BENOITE: No more struggle.

JOSEPH: (*indicating the tree*) It's supposed to come from far away...like me.

THE GRASS HAS YELLOWED

In the garden.

BENOITE: He wants to call me "Mother!"

FERNAND: Don't give in to him.

BENOITE: This morning, he went out very early.

FERNAND: Come on, you don't have to worry any longer...

BENOITE: He could let us know when he's going to be away... He behaves so strangely...

FERNAND: Like a living human being.

BENOITE: Of course...

FERNAND: To think that there are doctors who make mistakes like that!

BENOITE: Doctors never make mistakes, other people do. But if the tests *were* faulty, that means that today some boy who may actually be dying is being treated for a simple cold.

FERNAND: (*disturbed*) That's a possibility, but we can't worry about everyone, Benoîte.

A pause.

BENOITE: So! That's it for our Joseph.

FERNAND: Ah, yes! You want someone alive, *he's* alive all right! He's more alive than everyone else put together. He jumps over benches as he walks down the street. Camille told me that the old lady who sells those cheeses, the ones that are black like her dress, the one who smells like a goat—he threw his arms around her and kissed her.

BENOITE: He's going to make himself ridiculous.

FERNAND: We're the ones he's going to make ridiculous. He talks to trees. Yesterday, he swung up into an apple tree: "Hello, old friend, Eve sends her love." Tsk tsk tsk!

BENOITE: He should be told that fruit trees have fragile branches... What if he fell...

FERNAND: (*Looks suspiciously at Benoîte. A brief pause.*) I ran into that guy who used to sell the Party newspaper with you...

BENOITE: Hmmm...

FERNAND: ...the one who works in the shoe factory...

BENOITE: Yes?

FERNAND: He said that the cell...that right now they could sure use some of your pep and vigor.

BENOITE: So?

FERNAND: Nothing...nothing. That's it. (*Brief pause.*)

BENOITE: I used to get frostbite in the winter...

FERNAND: Party frostbite.

BENOITE: Don't *you* start talking that way...

FERNAND: (*tenderly*) What's the matter, Benoîte?

BENOITE: It's as though I were slipping...

FERNAND: Are you tired?

BENOITE: No, not at all...

FERNAND: Is it because of the miracle—

BENOITE: Let's try not to use the word "miracle," it's ridiculous. It's this roasting summer that's cooking everything...

FERNAND: It's just the same old summer up to its usual tricks...

BENOITE: We just sit here, without moving, leaning over the railing. We listen to the last flies of the summer, buzzing away. The grass is turning yellow. The stores are already putting winter clothes in the windows. The john is still leaking...

FERNAND: It's been forever...

BENOITE: The plumber is sick.

FERNAND: And our principles keep us from changing plumbers...

BENOITE: You can't abandon a man with viral hepatitis.

FERNAND: We're not going to invite him to convalesce in our bedroom.

Benoîte shrugs her shoulders.

FERNAND: Let's take a few days' vacation.

BENOITE: You don't know how glad I was that the Goudelkas postponed their visit till Christmas... I like them a lot. They're real artists. The lady next door said that this winter was going to be snowy, with lots of crows...

FERNAND: She's a little bit nuts, isn't she?

BENOITE: She's got her own way of talking. She says she'd had a whole "crud"—*crowd*—of misfortunes lately...

FERNAND: Well, I'm still sorry we didn't get to little Muguette's wedding. Wurtemberg, so picturesque, all ham and forget-me-nots.... My brother will never forgive me...

BENOITE: It's in Westphalia, the ham...and the forget-me-nots would have been over...

FERNAND: We talked about Greece.

BENOITE: Oh no! All those columns that have lost the temples they used to go with... And how can anyone live up to a country where the man at the garage is called Agamemnon and the girl who sells sandals is called Antigone.... I never saw Chloe so happy, so beside herself...

FERNAND: She's the one who brought him back.

BENOITE: We all did.... No, not even when we celebrated her fifteenth birthday with fireworks and a band in the garden...

FERNAND: That seems so long ago, that party...

BENOITE: It was last year.

FERNAND: So many things have happened since...

BENOITE: Only one thing, but that one vast as the sea...

FERNAND: Where does he get the money for all our presents...? He was poorer than Job...

BENOITE: When he got ill and we took him in he'd banked what he'd saved from his job at the factory to take a course. Chloe told me that he'd made arrangements for us to have the money when he died.

FERNAND: But now that he's alive it doesn't mean he shouldn't pay us back.

BENOITE: Pay us back? I don't want money.

FERNAND: Listen.... He gave me a fedora.

BENOITE: Which you never wear...

FERNAND: It's too new...and it never occurs to him to mention paying rent?

BENOITE: Let him get back on his feet.

FERNAND: The children won't have had any vacation...

BENOITE: He got a phone call this morning.

FERNAND: "He" called, and we'll pay for it.

BENOITE: He just replied yes, yes, yes and no, no, no...

FERNAND: You want me to interpret that?

BENOITE: I think I don't know him at all, in fact.

FERNAND: He plays great chess. And his naivete is obviously only a clever ploy. In any event, we ought to ask him for our room back. He could think of that for himself. We certainly do...

BENOITE: He's going to surprise us, have it re–papered.

FERNAND: What? He thinks he owns the place now! If it were up to me, I'd have it fumigated!

BENOITE: What a thing to say!

FERNAND: There's nothing nastier than a disease that suddenly abandons its victim...with no explanation.

BENOITE: We can't have it fumigated as long as he's still here.

FERNAND: Yes, and just how long is that going to be, in your estimation?

BENOITE: It's odd, but I haven't really been able to get back to sleeping normally. I'd become just like a young mother, waking at the slightest sound from his room.

FERNAND: Yes, and just how long is he going to stay here, in your opinion?

Benoîte gives Fernand a long look. Her gaze, neither interrogative nor responsive, freezes him.

FERNAND: (*to dispel his uneasiness*) You'll see, we'll all begin to live again.

BENOITE: Why, weren't you living?

FERNAND: I can admit it, now: no. I wasn't living. My hat was living, but I wasn't! But now, it's time to...

BENOITE: (*raising her head*) Look. The swallows are gathering.

FERNAND: Already?

BENOITE: It's going to be a harsh winter.

FERNAND: We're going to be able to have our friends over again: the good ones and the nutty ones and the old ones, the ones who like to drink and the ones who've given up drinking. Tsk, tsk, tsk. Right, Benoîte?

BENOITE: Yes, Fernand. Tsk, tsk, tsk. But not right away.

Camille enters.

CAMILLE: Have you seen what Joseph's doing? He's hoeing around the gooseberry bushes down at the bottom of the garden.

FERNAND: What does he think he's up to?

CAMILLE: You were going to do it!

FERNAND: I didn't ask *him* to!

CAMILLE: Yes, he's the only one in the family who does things without being asked.

FERNAND: I don't want anyone fooling with my garden without my permission.

CAMILLE: (*laughing*) Is that a new rule? Joseph's a good looking guy! And not only is he good looking, he's alive. When's the party going to be?

FERNAND: What party?

CAMILLE: First we were going to throw him a party to console him for dying, and then we were going to throw him one to congratulate him on living, and so far there's been nothing.

BENOITE: We'll give him his party. But couldn't we manage to act a little less frantically?

FERNAND: And are we going to have to talk about Joseph for the rest of our lives?

CAMILLE: (*taken aback*) What's got into you two?

BENOITE: I need some rest.

CAMILLE: Ever since Joseph has come back to life, so many good things have happened! Yesterday I got "taken up."

FERNAND: (*to Benoîte*) Taken up?

CAMILLE: And once I was up I was happy as a hen floating on eggs...

FERNAND: What is she talking about?

CAMILLE: Good Lord, you never listen to anything these days... I've been militating for them to let me for months.

BENOITE: Don't use the word "militate" so lightly.

CAMILLE: Lightly? On a crane, when for two years now that's all I've wanted?

FERNAND: She's going to be a crane operator?

CAMILLE: They all thought I wouldn't make it up there. But I'm very gifted. No dizziness at all. The precision of an astronaut. Incredibly calm.

FERNAND: A crane operator?

CAMILLE: During Friday's storm, there I was, swinging between the thunder and the lightning, it was super! I'd like to work at night, up among the stars.

FERNAND: What did the others say?

CAMILLE: I was up too high, I couldn't hear. With my cameras and microphones, up on the fifteenth floor, and the whole town down below me—I feel like a queen.

FERNAND: Was the moon full when we were producing her?

CAMILLE: To you it looks like I'm revolving in the sky, but the sky's really revolving around me... This doesn't move you at all, does it Benoîte...

BENOITE: (*dubiously*) No, no, it does... I'm very moved.

FERNAND: He didn't say whether he intended going soon now?

CAMILLE: Who?

FERNAND: Joseph.

CAMILLE: Go? Go where?

Fernand does not reply. Richard enters.

RICHARD: (*irritably*) The mother of my friend who committed suicide—she's getting married again.

BENOITE: Why shouldn't she?

RICHARD: He was buried just five months ago—he probably still has his blue eyes...does the color fade...right away?

BENOITE: You're beginning to annoy us, Richard, just "a bit."

RICHARD: And the thought of a woman moaning in ecstasy in the very house where her son...

BENOITE: Now you're annoying us "a lot."

RICHARD: Where's Joseph?

CAMILLE: Down in the gooseberry bushes...

RICHARD: I want him to explain what happens when the two kings come face to face...

FERNAND: Did he tell you he intended to leave soon?

RICHARD: Leave?

FERNAND: Yes, leave.

RICHARD: Why should he leave?

CAMILLE: Yesterday he scrubbed down the bathroom, the hall-ways, the johns...

BENOITE: If I needed a cleaning woman, I'd say so.

FERNAND: And I suppose that gives him the right to eat three times what we do!

Camille and Richard exchange astonished looks.

RICHARD: When a person comes back to life, he needs to catch up on the time he has lost.

FERNAND: When a person comes back to life he's not called upon to mess around in other people's lives!

CAMILLE: He's no bother...

RICHARD: He's even fixed our old swing...

FERNAND: One wonders whatever for?

CAMILLE: And always whistling. He whistles like people used to do in the old socialist films, the ones you like so much, Benoîte...Mother.

BENOITE: The tunes he whistles are so vulgar!... And, unlike you, I don't find him all that charming...

CAMILLE: You used to say he was an angel.

BENOITE: An angel!? The word isn't part of my vocabulary.

RICHARD: Correct me if I'm wrong: isn't Joseph the boy you said you'd love until death?

FERNAND: And for whom we gave up a wedding, Wurtemberg, the Goudelkas, our vacation in Greece.

CAMILLE: September's the time to go to Greece. The tourists are gone. There's only Greece.

FERNAND: That's enough joking. You do realize that we can't go on keeping a perfectly healthy young man!

CAMILLE: His being healthy doesn't upset me.

RICHARD: Or me.

CAMILLE: Nor does his taking care of the garden, cleaning, doing the shopping...

FERNAND: Maybe you think we should be paying him like a gardener, a cleaning lady, an errand boy?

RICHARD: He doesn't ask anything...

FERNAND: He does worse: he expects.

RICHARD: What's got into you all of a sudden?

FERNAND: All of a sudden? He's been well for two months now...and nothing!

BENOITE: Tomorrow we'll all have lunch in the garden, it will be easier to talk to him, among the flowers.

CAMILLE: Talk to him about what?

FERNAND: We've got to make up our minds.

RICHARD: About what?

FERNAND: To remain together.

RICHARD: But we are together.

CAMILLE: When you used to see us all, so good looking, so intelligent, you always used to tell Fernand that you were sorry you hadn't had six children...

BENOITE: I'm not sorry now.

Silence.

RICHARD: I signed up for boxing lessons.

FERNAND: Why did you do that?

BENOITE: To get your nose broken.

CAMILLE: It might suit him.

RICHARD: I want to be a professional.

FERNAND: It's not a profession.

RICHARD: You're right. It's an art.

FERNAND: The whole business is run by crooks.

RICHARD: What isn't? That's what attracts me—the thought of punching out some crook, injustice, indifference...

FERNAND: You've got your work cut out for you.

RICHARD: While you're sitting with your feet up in your living room you'll be able to hear me, floating like a butterfly, stinging like a bee...

BENOITE: And when you've gone blind?

RICHARD: I'll fight blind opponents. (*A pause.*) In any event, as far as Joseph is concerned, he's fine right here with us.

CAMILLE: And so are we.

FERNAND: Are you going to feed him?

RICHARD: When you start feeding a child when he's twenty, he won't have cost any more in the end. You wanted someone to help you with the second–hand business...

FERNAND: He doesn't know anything about it.

RICHARD: And I suppose I do?

FERNAND: I'd have broken you in.

RICHARD: Why not him?

FERNAND: He's not my son.

RICHARD: You can only work with a family member? But I thought you loved him like a son.

FERNAND: Yes, like a son.

RICHARD: But sons, real sons, are the ones you make, not the ones you love.

FERNAND: (*to Benoîte*) What's he trying to say?

RICHARD: You loved him like you love a funeral wreath.

BENOITE: Richard, shut up.

CAMILLE: Look, he's gathering quince. Will you make us some jelly, Benoîte?

FERNAND: By God, he really makes himself at home, doesn't he!?

CAMILLE: Where else should he think he is? Come on, Richard, let's go help him.

>   *They exit.*

FERNAND: Now you see where uncontrollable compassion can lead.

BENOITE: You all make me tired.

FERNAND: I'm always the one who has to deal with things. (*A pause.*) Would you like some tea?

BENOITE: What good would that do?

WHAT DOES JOSEPH SAY?

FERNAND: Sit down, Chloe; we want to talk to you. (*Pause.*) What does Joseph say?

CHLOE: He's going around in a dream. He can't believe in it.

BENOITE: We believe in it.

FERNAND: We believe in it every day. We've believed in it now for two months.

BENOITE: We rejoiced, Chloe, we're still rejoicing.

FERNAND: We never stop rejoicing.

CHLOE: (*who has not yet understood*) Yes...so do I.

BENOITE: We don't regret anything we've done.

FERNAND: It isn't everyone who would have given so freely, like we have... Tsk tsk tsk...

BENOITE: Without a second thought, with all the patience of people who love...

CHLOE: I know. And I'm proud of you.

FERNAND: Now, however, we've reached what you might call the post–rejoicing stage...

CHLOE: Which means...?

FERNAND: Just what's on his mind, Joseph?

CHLOE: (*Taken aback, she searches for the right word.*) Jubilation...

FERNAND: Yes, of course...

CHLOE: What's worrying you?

FERNAND: You introduced him to us. We trusted you completely.

CHLOE: You were right...

BENOITE: It's not your fault, Chloe. But you've got to understand that everything's changed.

CHLOE: You're frightening me...

Brief pause.

FERNAND: When does he intend to go away?

CHLOE: Go away?

FERNAND: Yes, go away. Leave the house.

CHLOE: I don't know...

FERNAND: He doesn't talk to you about it?

CHLOE: ...No...

FERNAND: So it's up to us to make his mind up for him.

CHLOE: Are you upset that he's been cured?

BENOITE: We're upset.

FERNAND: But we're not going to go on being upset for the rest of our lives.

CHLOE: He's got a wonderful life ahead of him now.

BENOITE: So let him get on with his wonderful life...

FERNAND: But let him get on with it somewhere else...

CHLOE: When he was sick his presence didn't bother you.

BENOITE: That was because of his disease.

FERNAND: He came here to die. (*Pause.*) Yes or no?

CHLOE: ...Yes...

BENOITE: That contract between us has now become invalid.

CHLOE: (*to Benoîte*) You loved him like a son...

BENOITE: I still love him. Even if he's not exactly the same son...the same man, I should say...

CHLOE: He's the same, but now he's healthy too. Isn't living even more wonderful?

BENOITE: There's nothing more wonderful than life. Nothing greater. Nothing more sparkling. There's nothing else.

CHLOE: Live young people matter more than dead ones.

BENOITE: All that matters is one's word. When he came here to us he was slipping off into the unknown. We promised to go with him all the way. Now he's pulled out of it. We don't know how. That's fine. That's perfect for him. But we *could* say that he didn't keep his word...

CHLOE: Mother...

BENOITE: ...that he didn't keep his word. And that in a manner of speaking he deceived us...

CHLOE: But mother, what are you saying?

FERNAND: Did he ever tell you that there was a chance he might get well?

CHLOE: How could he? The hospital didn't keep anything from him. He was incurable. He was on the brink of dying. Nobody can explain why the diagnosis changed.

FERNAND: And it could change again, for that matter, why not? Just don't let him have a relapse; we'll have no relapses here.

CHLOE: How can you say that?

FERNAND: How can he just move in...

Pause.

CHLOE: I'll never be able to love you now like I did before.

BENOITE: Of course you'll love us—don't whine.

CHLOE: I was so proud of you, Mother.

BENOITE: You may be again. But, you see, even kindness has its shortcomings. Kindness is like a horse: it sees everything magnified eight times.

CHLOE: And you liked seeing his death magnified.

BENOITE: No, it was the difficulty.

CHLOE: And Joseph's brand–new life is too large?

BENOITE: Forty times too large. His "brand–new life" is crushing me... his good health overwhelms me...his gaiety is oppressive... He moves like a tank. He sings like a fog horn. He's all over the place. He's stifling us.

FERNAND: Real charity begins at home. And it ends at home. Real charity works in a closed circuit. Otherwise there's nothing but disorder and waste.

CHLOE: I'm sorry for you.

FERNAND: You're right to feel sorry for us. Thanks to him we've done without Germany, we've lost our friends from the East, our appetite, our vacations, Greece, sleep... And we've been shut up in the pantry. Don't you think it's time we thought about ourselves?

CHLOE: I thought that "ourselves" was him too.

FERNAND: Give me one good reason why we should keep him?

CHLOE: For happiness.

BENOITE: To each his own, Chloe.

FERNAND: The boy has never been anything but an illusion, a trompe–l'oeil.

CHLOE: If you want to punish him for not dying, it would be better to kill him.

FERNAND: *(to Benoîte, referring to Chloe's remark)* There you see how irrational acts of rescue can end up.

CHLOE: Where do you want him to go?

BENOITE: When you're healthy the world's your oyster.

CHLOE: Let him catch his breath.

FERNAND: His breath? Oh, that's something he's got plenty of! We got him out of dying. Now let him get out of the house.

BEING HAPPY

FERNAND: You're a very good chess player, Joseph.

JOSEPH: Thanks.

FERNAND: But so am I. Well, here you are, back in the land of the living. What are you planning on doing?

JOSEPH: Being happy.

FERNAND: Of course. And then?

JOSEPH: Learning how to stay happy.

FERNAND: Of course...of course...

JOSEPH: That word, "living," you know, I can't quite take it in. It's larger than life...

FERNAND: Of course, certainly. Certainly, but...

JOSEPH: Yes?

FERNAND: Where will you go?

JOSEPH: When?

FERNAND: I'm not making myself clear. When are you going?

JOSEPH: Oh, don't worry. I'm not going away.

FERNAND: You're not...

JOSEPH: You think I'm the kind of ingrate who just says, "Thanks a lot, stay well, bye-bye"....

FERNAND: It's just...

JOSEPH: No, no. I can't imagine anything that would make me leave. (*Laughing*) Unless it would be you!

FERNAND: *(taken aback)* Natural...ly. But look, up until now, "here"—for you—was "*here*," if you know what I mean...but since then, I mean, "here," there's always afterwards...a year afterwards, to be exact, and so "here" isn't "here" any longer... Tsk tsk tsk!

JOSEPH: Later, much much later... I swear, I'll always be with you...

FERNAND: I mean, look, when I say "here," I mean "our" house.

JOSEPH: Yes, "our" house.

FERNAND: Listen, Joseph. Listen carefully to what I'm trying to say to you. Let's be clear. We are a family, and in that family...

JOSEPH: And there, in that family, I was born... Before you, I was nothing. Lost. An orphan. Lost in the clouds. Books, all books, were hard for me. Every city was a prison. I met Chloe. You took me in, the fatal disease turned out to be heaven–sent. A gift of God. It let me be born again. It gave me a real family, with sisters and brothers. And now I'm well. Saved. Happy... I've never told you that before.

FERNAND: Joseph, I was thinking that...

JOSEPH: I'll try never to give you cause for concern. I'm all yours. How could I put asunder what death itself could not put asunder?

FERNAND: Joseph... I *have* three children...

JOSEPH: No, four. Benoîte's right: you don't know how to count.

FERNAND: I'm just a pawn, obviously...

JOSEPH: Speaking of that, the next time we play I'll have to explain the difference between a major pawn and a minor pawn... A storm's coming up... I'm going to finish gathering the quinces... They're bigger than grapefruit. It will have been a wonderful summer...

He runs off.

FERNAND: Either the boy's an idiot or he's extremely clever and I've been had once again.

Chloe crosses. Fernand goes to her quickly. He speaks to her but we don't hear...the rain and storm have already begun.

\

ALL THESE WORDS IN THE NIGHT

JOSEPH: What's happening? I saw suitcases...are your parents going on holiday?

CHLOE: We're all going. Fernand is taking us to the seaside.

JOSEPH: I haven't got a suitcase.

CHLOE: You don't need one.

JOSEPH: (*laughing*) That's true enough. I've only got my jeans...

CHLOE: Joseph, you're not going.

JOSEPH: You want me to look after the house?

CHLOE: (*carefully*) No, Joseph. To leave it.

JOSEPH: Why?

CHLOE: It's all over.

> *Silence.*

JOSEPH: They liked me so much...

CHLOE: They liked you a lot.

JOSEPH: A family like yours, I thought it would last a lifetime.

CHLOE: Joseph, you're cured.

JOSEPH: I tell myself that every minute. At night, I wake up with joy.

CHLOE: You're cured, Joseph. But...you're not one of the family.

> *Pause.*

JOSEPH: I was ashamed of my father. Of his being poor. Of his bad health. Of his job. I was ashamed of being ashamed and of his threadbare coat...

CHLOE: That's all a long time ago, forgotten...

JOSEPH: Yes, I had forgotten. I'm being punished...

CHLOE: No. It's just that things have changed...

JOSEPH: (*almost cheerfully*) And yet, I no longer worry you.

CHLOE: You worry us more than before. That's another reason you must leave. (*Short pause.*)

JOSEPH: Where will I go?

CHLOE: Wherever you like, Joseph.

JOSEPH: "Wherever you like" isn't a place. (*Pause.*) That's all right. I'll make out. And in two years I'll come back for you.

CHLOE: No, Joseph.

JOSEPH: You think I'll forget you?

CHLOE: In two years, I won't be the same.

JOSEPH: I'll love you even if you aren't the same.

CHLOE: Don't say that...

JOSEPH: Why?

CHLOE: And don't come back.

JOSEPH: And all the things we said to each other, at night, there in the house?

CHLOE: I loved you then. I thought about you all the time. In the mornings, when there was a storm, I used to call your name into the wind. Sometimes the wind was so strong that your name would be blown back into my throat, and that was delicious...

JOSEPH: And today?

CHLOE: Today, I can't see anything. I don't know anything. And even... I don't see you. I never deceived you, Joseph...

JOSEPH: I know...

CHLOE: But I'm worn out. I wanted you to live with all my strength...

JOSEPH: I'll wait. We'll be together again.

CHLOE: It would be like going backwards...with our eyes closed. All that seems like a hundred years ago. Why didn't you make love to me?

JOSEPH: You were so serious. So young. And I was so wrapped up in myself. Under guard...(*Silence.*) When are you leaving?

CHLOE: Tomorrow evening.

JOSEPH: So soon! We mustn't be afraid. I would have liked to...

Chloe gestures him not to go on.

JOSEPH: (*with his own special smile*) I was already starting to like my room with the geraniums.

CHLOE: Listen, Joseph. (*She is trying not to weaken—she stops.*)

JOSEPH: What happened, actually?

CHLOE: Something glowed. I held you in my arms. I asked you to live, and you did it.

JOSEPH: I did it... Don't be sad, Chloe. You're the one who brought me into the world. (*He puts a small box in her hands.*) It's a ring, not worth much, really. But wear it for a few days...and then, when you're out there...throw it into the waves...some day some boy will find it.... And before you leave, just say my name once more...

CHLOE: Joseph...

JOSEPH: That's fine. I'll hear it for a long, long time.

CHLOE: And in spite of everything, we've won.

JOSEPH: Yes; we've won.

EPILOGUE

Suitcases and bags. Joseph, in great distress, looks around the place he has loved. He runs his hand over various objects.

FERNAND: Are you still here? Are you ever going to understand? Your imaginary convalescence from your imaginary disease has lasted long enough. It's over. Finished. Done with. So off you go. Disappear. Calmly, quietly, without a word and without looking back.

JOSEPH: It's true...I hadn't understood...

BENOITE: (*entering*) Should I shut the attic?

FERNAND: Of course.

BENOITE: The skylight?

FERNAND: That too. (*Benoîte exits.*) What were you expecting— you can spit it out.

JOSEPH: I wasn't expecting anything. I was happy.

FERNAND: And you thought that we, simple tools that we are, were going to let ourselves be saddled with a boy like you for the rest of our lives, a boy without a future, without any money, without a profession and completely healthy...just because he was *happy*? We're a family. We're a family that I've created, by traveling, by putting two and two together, and it's a thing well done...

BENOITE: (*returning*) The skylight...what if it rains?

FERNAND: It won't. (*Benoîte exits.*) This family has been constructed. And it's no use prowling around it...it'll do you no good to hoe around the gooseberry bushes, because that kind of prowler I just tell to fuck off...understand?

BENOITE: (*returning*) And the cat? And the kittens?

FERNAND: What do you mean, the cat and the kittens?

BENOITE: We can't take them with us...who's going to feed them?

FERNAND: (*to Joseph*) Oh no! I'm onto you! First you feed the cat and then you offer to gather up the chestnuts. (*To Benoîte*) Ask the lady next door. (*Benoîte exits.*) You were supposed to die. You got well. You did all you could do to accomplish that. Perfect. So pass your secret on to others. What more do you want? Let me be very frank: You're going to remove yourself from our property and you're going to leave Chloe alone. She's just a child.

JOSEPH: I'll never see her again.

FERNAND: Let's not get sentimental, okay?

JOSEPH: I don't know any of you...

FERNAND: But we've learned to know you...

BENOITE: (*returning*) The lady next door is allergic to cat hair.

FERNAND: She's doing it on purpose, the old grouch!

BENOITE: She'll come to feed them, but she says she'll have to do it very quickly. (*Benoîte exits.*)

FERNAND: Do you know what I think you are? I think you're an usurper. An invader. Your illness was all a fabrication, made up...

JOSEPH: Don't say that. I was so sick... I was condemned...

FERNAND: That was just something you made up to get to Chloe, marry her and move in.

JOSEPH: Throw me out if you must, but don't say things...

FERNAND: When a person is as sick as you were supposed to be, they die. If they get well, they know why. Nothing in your story holds water, and now...here...you're a threat...

JOSEPH: A threat?

FERNAND: We never asked where you came from. You were sick, sick people have no past.

JOSEPH: And a living person has too much?

FERNAND: A survivor like you, yes.

BENOITE: (*agitated and distracted. She seems to have aged. She has dressed for the trip.*) We'd better be careful not to miss the train...

FERNAND: Come on, Benoîte...we're taking the car. (*To Joseph*) Maybe you thought...

BENOITE: (*absently*) ... careful not to miss the car...

CHLOE: Mother, Camille took my suitcase. What shall I do?

BENOITE: What about hers?

CHLOE: She has two suitcases, two knapsacks and a kind of bag...

FERNAND: She might as well bring her crane too.

BENOITE: I'll be right there. (*Exits with Chloe.*)

FERNAND: You probably thought life was like a field of for-get–me–nots.

JOSEPH: No, life for me wasn't even a single forget–me–not.

FERNAND: Don't preach. You've already given us that perfor-mance, and it's gone on far too long. (*Violently*) So now, offstage and away with you. Tsk! Tsk! Tsk!

BENOITE: (*returning*) You can say what you have to say without shouting, without getting angry...

FERNAND: Tsk! Tsk! Tsk!

JOSEPH: Excuse me.... For living.

FERNAND: Get the suitcases. Call the children...

JOSEPH: (*moving towards Benoîte*) Goodbye Mo—...ma'am. I'll always remember you.

BENOITE: (*Hesitates and then kisses him.*) Goodbye, Joseph. A person has to learn how far they can go...

JOSEPH: I will... (*He backs off.*) I'm beginning to...

FERNAND: And you said he looked like an angel. I'd like to know where you get your angels from! (*Once again overcome with anger*) Let him go! Let him disappear! Let him fly away! Tsk! Tsk! Tsk! And let us forget him!

BENOITE: It's done, Fernand. I'll go help Chloe. (*As she exits she passes Camille, carrying a load of baggage.*) You're always afraid of forgetting something, my girl... (*She exits.*)

FERNAND: My poor Camille, we're not going to Tibet!

CAMILLE: What do I hear? So it wasn't just a joke! That young man we've taken in, fed, bathed, is still refusing to die according to the terms of his contract? He's made us all suffer for nothing. Really, kids today don't know what honor is, their word doesn't mean a thing, they've got no manners! He's content just to live, young as he is...just like all of us.

FERNAND: (*trying to ignore her*) Where are you going?

CAMILLE: Somewhere else.

FERNAND: Is it far?

CAMILLE: Even farther.

FERNAND: An experiment?

CAMILLE: A conclusion. You can't go on living with parents who no longer resemble the ones you used to love.

FERNAND: Up there on your crane, with all your twenty years, you're in a great position to judge good and evil.

CAMILLE: Up on my crane I'm ashamed of you, Fernand. I'm ashamed for all of us. I didn't know that goodness was more dangerous than hatred and that in our house goodness was surrounded with conditions, a goodness meted out, bit by bit. If you can't manage to do it totally, all at once, then it's better to keep it in your pocket. The same pocket you keep your revolver in... (*She exits.*)

FERNAND: I'm going to kill her, with her crane and her fine words! (*Shouting*) Benoîte! Benoîte! (*Benoîte returns, followed by Chloe.*) Where's Richard?

CHLOE: He left this morning at sunrise.

FERNAND: (*in a low voice*) Tsk! Tsk! Tsk!

CHLOE: He did leave a letter.

She hands it to Benoîte.

Fernand gently takes the letter from Benoîte and puts it in his pocket.

BENOITE: (*in tears*) You never know... You never know at all... You never do... (*She gets hold of herself, as usual.*) When we come back from the seaside, I'm going to go back to the Party...

A pause.

FERNAND: Why have they left?

BENOITE: Normal children do leave.

FERNAND: Like that?

BENOITE: Like that, or some other way.

FERNAND: (*upset*) So let's go, too.

> *The three of them sadly pick up their suitcases, and as they are preparing to cross the threshold Mrs. Ronsard enters, out of breath, frightened...*

MRS. RONSARD: Oh my God. My God! It's really not your day! You're about to leave...but you can't leave now. Fortunately you haven't left yet. My God...leaving! You think you're going to leave and then fate hits you like a ton of bricks. It happened down at the plant market, where they sell the shrubs. Your protégé, your Joseph, that's his name isn't it, all of a sudden I saw him and then all of a sudden I didn't... He'd fallen down, he'd collapsed face down on the ground. He'd almost stopped breathing. Then the ambulance came. Oh my God! It only took about four minutes, the ambulance...

BENOITE: Is he at the hospital?

MRS. RONSARD: That's where he is.

> *A pause.*

CHLOE: Do they know anything?

MRS. RONSARD: No one knows anything. But the orderlies covered him up with the sheet.

> *Silence.*

BENOITE: So that does it for the vacation. Let's unpack...

FERNAND: (*distraught*) No, let's go. Please. Let's go anyway. (*They look at him.*) Let's still go.

They pick up their suitcases and exit.

MRS. RONSARD: (*alone, in tears*) I'll look after the cat and the kittens...

Blackout.

～